Becoming Two-Spirit

Becoming Two-Spirit
*Gay Identity and Social Acceptance
in Indian Country*

Brian Joseph Gilley

University of Nebraska Press
Lincoln and London

Part of chapter 5 appeared in earlier form in
"Making Traditional Spaces: Cultural Compro-
mise at Two-Spirit Gatherings in Oklahoma,"
American Indian Culture and Research Journal 28,
no. 2 (2004): 81–96, and is reprinted by permis-
sion of the American Indian Studies Center, UCLA
© Regents of the University of California. Part of
chapter 5 also appeared as "Two-Spirit Powwows
and the Search for Social Acceptance in Indian
Country," in *Powwow*, edited by Clyde Ellis, Luke
Eric Lassiter, and Gary H. Dunham, 224–40
(Lincoln: University of Nebraska Press, 2005).

Book designed and typeset in Minion and Trinité
by R. Eckersley.

Library of Congress Cataloging-in-Publication Data

Gilley, Brian Joseph, 1972–
Becoming two-spirit : gay identity and social
acceptance in Indian country / Brian Joseph Gilley.
p.   cm.
Includes bibliographical references and index.
ISBN-13: 978-0-8032-7126-5 (pbk. : alk. paper)
ISBN-10: 0-8032-7126-3 (pbk. : alk. paper)
1. Indian gays—North America. 2. Homosexuality,
Male—North America. I. Title.
E98.S48G55 2006   306.76'6208997—dc22
2006006956

For Patrick

CONTENTS

Preface

I did not set out to write a book about Two-Spirit men and social acceptance. Rather, the research for this project began as an interest in how Native peoples were dealing with the HIV/AIDS epidemic. The focus changed the first evening I went to a meeting of the Green Country Two-Spirit Society, whose official mission is to design and implement HIV/AIDS prevention programming for urban Native men who have sex with men. Besides the discomfort of being an outsider in such a small community, what struck me the most about that first meeting was that very few of the men were talking about HIV/AIDS in any direct personal way, nor were they talking openly about their experiences with the epidemic. Instead, I found a diverse group of men who all shared several concerns that I thought at the time only peripherally related to HIV/AIDS – they were all Native, all identified as gay or bisexual, and all felt as if their sexuality had at one time or another pitted them against their families and their tribal communities. After attending only a few meetings of the group I realized that these men simply looked at HIV/AIDS as a part of being gay in America. No doubt for them HIV/AIDS was a tragic disease and had affected Indians in very specific ways, but they approached it in a matter-of-fact way that reflected its presence in their everyday lives. But what concerned the men the most was the fact that they felt socially and personally separated from their families and communities because of their sexuality. They knew full well, through direct experience or listening to fellow Natives talk, that their sexuality was a source of shame and disdain. They also feared homophobia so much that it often kept them from participating in the social and spiritual practices that their families taught them were so important to their Native identity. It was not until much later in my research that I discovered that the alienation the men feel could be linked to the reasons that Native GLBT people put themselves at risk for HIV/AIDS. In order to address this link I felt that I had to tackle the issue of alienation and self- and social acceptance first. Therefore, it is

the relationship between constructions of Two-Spirit identity and social acceptance with which this book is primarily concerned.

Once I committed to researching Two-Spirit identity, the men of the
Green Country Two-Spirit Society and the Two-Spirit Society of Denver gracefully accepted my continual presence. Besides being grateful to
them for allowing me to participate in their activities, record what they
said, and write about them, I am grateful that they did not hide their
feelings and that they let me into both the good and bad aspects of their
lives. Because I am not a gay man, many of the men felt that they were
taking a risk by allowing me to hang around and write about them. I
know that many of the men in both the Green Country and Denver
societies were apprehensive about my presence. Many of the men
speculated that I was a man "on the down low" (a straight man secretly
participating in gay sex and gay popular culture), that I was just having
trouble admitting that I was gay, or that I was researching "sexual devi-
ance." Interest in my sexual orientation faded but only after a few intense confrontations. On one occasion I was at a gay bar with members
of the Two-Spirit Society of Denver when one of the members loudly
confronted me, saying "What the hell do you care about gay people?
Why the hell is some straight guy doing research with gay Indian
people? To figure out what's wrong with us?" I replied with a stock answer about attempting to explain why gay Native American men were
forming alternative communities to deal with their alienation from
tribal society. However, this solicited only more rage from the somewhat intoxicated individual. I do not know that I ever provided satisfac-
tory answers to these kinds of questions, but I hope that the men of
these two societies see the results within this book as worth taking a
chance on me.

Despite my attempts to lessen the issue of my own sexuality in the
writing of this book, it kept resurfacing in comments from colleagues
and those who read the initial manuscript (and in many ways necessi-
tated the writing of this preface). Everyone who looked at the manuscript demanded that I position myself within the text, which translated to "Is the author speaking from a gay experiential point of view?"
Once I was identified as not gay within the manuscript, one reader felt

that it was good that "a straight person" was writing about a topic that had been marginalized within anthropology and that the positioning of my sexual orientation would provide a different perspective on the topic "and give such topics more credibility." The reader was commenting on the assumptions that many academics hold – that any book written about GLBT people (or any underrepresented group for that matter) by a member of that community is more a reflection of personal politics than scholarship. For this reason, it was not uncommon to have people I know say "Is there something you need to tell me?" upon hearing my research topic. The assumption in academia often seems to be that someone who is researching gay topics must be gay and only writing out of self-interest.

A friend and colleague pointed out that a straight person writing about GLBT people had the potential to challenge the "ghettoization" of studies on GLBT topics. At the same time, she felt it was problematic to assume that a straight person showing an interest in a GLBT topic would give it more legitimacy. She was troubled by the assumption that GLBT studies would only be legitimate once a non-gay person showed an interest. I agree with my colleague, and I also think it is unfortunate that in our society issues of sexual orientation lead to the necessity of my justifying an interest. It was not until I read the introduction of Don Kulick's insightful book *Travesti* that I came to recognize the importance of "coming out" to the readers of this book. Kulick recognizes that his sexual orientation gave him a certain legitimacy among his gay male transgender informants and no doubt added to the level of trust he enjoyed living among the *travesti*. I also had to admit that more than any other aspect of my personhood, sexuality affected my access to certain aspects of Two-Spirit men's lives, whether they trusted me or not, and whether the information in this book would be seen by my peers as another piece of literature celebrating gayness in America or a serious ethnographic study. My goal was to produce the latter.

In keeping with my goals as a scholar and ethnographer, this book focuses on the ways Two-Spirit men see themselves as subject to power-laden social relationships surrounding their sexual identity. Readers will notice an emphasis on a particular picture of Two-Spirit identity.

This emphasis comes from the men represented in the book. I will not claim that this book represents all GLBT Natives or all conceptions of Two-Spirit identity, nor do I endorse a particular conception of Two-Spiritedness. Rather, the book is focused on how I witnessed Two-Spirit men negotiate their identity as gay and Native among the difficulties of identifying oneself with both of these contested identities.

I have conceptualized the negotiation of the identities gay and Indian, as well as their manifestation in Two-Spirit identity, as *becoming*. The theme of becoming is something I witnessed over the course of the four years I actively interviewed and recorded information about Two-Spirit men and is the inspiration for the title of this book. Becoming, as I see it, best describes the ways I saw men openly battle with other Indian people over their alienation, adapt to racism among non-Indians and their own people, reconcile with their families, noticeably gain self-acceptance or continue to destroy themselves, and even a few pass on to the next world. All these experiences are enfolded into the men's conceptions of Two-Spirit identity and thus make it not only a term but also a form of personhood. For many of the men, coming to terms with life's difficulties was at the same time *becoming Two-Spirit*.

Acknowledgments

I owe a great deal to the men of the Green Country Two-Spirit Society and the Two-Spirit Society of Denver. Although they go unnamed for their own protection, I have thanked them personally and "in the right way." In particular I would like to thank the people whom I have named – Ben, Sheila, Glen, Mick, and Andy – in the book. Although their identities are disguised, their contribution is not. I would like to especially thank Ben for teaching me not only about Two-Spirit people but also a lot about myself. Sheila was also extremely helpful in explaining the subtleties of Two-Spirit social relations and also in guiding me through Native American culture and gay society.

Three individuals were particularly important in the writing of this book and also in my development as a scholar. They are Morris Foster, Circe Sturm, and Margaret Bender. Morris Foster was a supportive doctoral committee chair and provided needed structure and grounding to my more extravagant ideas. I am grateful to Circe Sturm for energizing my interest in anthropology when I was not sure about continuing. I am grateful to Margaret Bender for introducing me to the importance of gender in intellectual inquiry and for always being a source of critical perspective. Besides their intellectual contributions, all three of these scholars endeared themselves to me with their generosity of time and friendship. I also would like to thank Birgit Hans, Barbara Handy-Marchello, and Merry Ketterling, all of whom gave me their critical input on various aspects of the manuscript and research, which no doubt make it much better. I would also like to thank my colleagues at the University of Vermont for their support: John Gennari for being supportive, Deborah Blom for being encouraging, and her husband, Jeff Clarke, for teaching me how to cross-country ski, Luis Vivanco for reading parts of the manuscript with a critical eye, and J. Dickinson for recommending source material and commentary on my ideas. I also thank Rob Gordon, Michael Sheridan, and Jeanne Shea for their support. I thank Jim Petersen for always taking the time to listen to my rambling ideas. His untimely and tragic death has been difficult to grasp. He will be dearly missed.

Thanks also go to Nancy Cahwee, Dannette MacIntosh, Karl and Patty Beaston, Gary Holmes, and William Ray. My appreciation goes to Jack Weinstein and Kim Donehower for their friendship, humor, and irony. I would also like to thank the staff at the University of Nebraska Press. My gratitude goes especially to Gary Dunham who believed in the potential of the manuscript and taught me how to write a book.

My family has remained steadfastly supportive throughout this process. I would like to thank my parents, Jo Ann and Gary Gilley, who have always encouraged my interest in anthropology and whose pride in my accomplishments keeps me motivated. I would like to thank my grandmother Joy Gilley and the rest of my family who wondered what I was working on all this time. I would especially like to thank my sister Jennifer Gilley-Brooks, who always is there to listen and provide humor. I thank Chris Brooks for his support in the outdoors. Mike and Georgene Dwyer were supportive during the research and writing process and continue to honor me with their continued interest. Sara Dwyer, George Lane, and Claire and Josh Lee have listened to my endless explanations, which helped me stay familiar with the work and my ideas. My daughter, Aurianna, continues to inspire me with her intellectual curiosity, humor, and love. She helps me to not take all this too seriously. I am grateful to my infant son, Parker, for keeping me optimistic. Caroline, my wife, has read this manuscript more times than anyone and was always kind in her corrections and suggestions. More importantly, she has supported me throughout this process with her love and understanding. I am forever grateful.

CHAPTER ONE

Seeking Self- and Social Acceptance

Any illusions I had about reaching that moment in an ethnographer's fieldwork when the host population considers you "one of them" came crashing down when I was relegated to the "straight men's room." I had been conducting research on Two-Spirit (gay American Indian) men for not quite a year.[1] I was visiting Denver, Colorado, to conduct interviews with Two-Spirit men and to attend the Denver March Powwow. Sheila, a key consultant, traveled with me to Denver to see old friends and dance in the powwow. The two people we were staying with, Glen and Pete, were close friends of Sheila's and had opened their home to any and all comers who needed a place to stay during the powwow. It turned out that 15 people ended up staying with Glen and Pete, including three Polish exchange students who came with Sheila's cousin from the Rosebud Indian Reservation. The three Polish men were on a "trip of curiosity," as they put it, visiting various Indian reservations in the United States, and Sheila's cousin Greg was their host at Rosebud. Greg thought it would be beneficial for them to visit the Denver March Powwow, seeing as it is one of the largest and best attended in the West.

When Sheila and I arrived at Glen and Pete's place, I was told with a snicker that I was staying in the back room with the "other straight guys," the Polish exchange students. Upon opening the door to the room I was hit with the nauseatingly pungent odor of unwashed human beings. I turned and walked back to the living room carrying my luggage with an obvious look of "no way" on my face. Attempting to contain his laughter, Glen handed me a bottle of Febreze air freshener and informed me that "only queens" were staying "out here" in the living room. I reluctantly went back to the room and placed my sleeping bag near the open window. Unfortunately, the three Polish men were fulfilling American stereotypes about the personal hygiene habits of Europeans. The Two-Spirit men sitting on the couches and the floor burst out laughing as I emerged from the bedroom. Sheila greeted my look of obvious disappointment with the living arrangements by telling me, "You're one of them, so the smell shouldn't bother you. All you straight men smell the same," followed by a burst of laughter from the other men.

I sulked the rest of the evening at the opening night of the powwow. When we returned to Glen and Pete's place, the men began getting ready to go on a circuit of the local gay clubs. As everyone gathered by the door, I noticed that people were acting weird. Sheila, who was for-ever cluing me in to cultural hints and appropriate behavior, suggested that I might want to hang out at the bookstore café down the street, since they have a "nice Native American book section." I finally caught on to Sheila's direction and opted to hang out around the house instead of going along. The Polish students actually never went to the powwow, but instead spent most of the weekend hanging out in the local techno dance bars. However, the presence of their lingering odor in the room was a continual point of humor and incited a seemingly endless bout of teasing me.

During that stay in Denver, all gladly granted me interviews, were generous with their time, explaining various aspects of their lives, and invited me to attend a Two-Spirit directed house ceremony and dinner. But I never quite got over the sting of the segregated sleeping arrange-ments and being excluded from "the fun." On the drive back to Okla-homa, I asked Sheila why I had been kept away. "Not everyone there knows you, and they don't know what you're going to write," she re-plied. "Maybe they don't want you to write about their sex lives or see-ing them drunk. Maybe they don't trust you like some of the other Two-Spirits you know. You know you aren't one of us, so why would you want to go out with us anyway?" she continued. "Or maybe," she said, "they want you to see what it's like to not feel totally welcome all the time. They are testing you."

Over the course of the five years I spent interviewing, hanging out with, and becoming friends with Two-Spirit men, I figured out that they were continually testing me, testing each other, and testing the boundaries of American Indian identity. Testing boundaries is a con-stant theme in Two-Spirit men's efforts to look for and locate self- and social acceptance amid the potential homophobia among their tribal communities, families, and non-gay Indians in general. By examining the ways Two-Spirit men test the boundaries of two seemingly solidified identities, gay and Indian, I seek to examine *why* they confront the limitations on the expression of individual and group-identity consciousness. Simply put, why do Two-Spirit men so desperately desire to be accepted by other Native peoples who have little or no tolerance for gender difference and same-sex relations? This book seeks to answer the questions of why Two-Spirit men attempt to reconcile a forced divide in their social worlds and how they reach their sense of who they are amid contemporary ideas about American Indian identity and culture.

Are There Gay Indians?

When I arrived at the gay pride parade and picnic sponsored by the "Oklahoma Pride Center," people were setting up tents, tables, and beer stands around the perimeter of the park. Within an hour a sizeable crowd accumulated to await the parade that would pass along the street adjacent to the park. Protestors lined the sidewalk opposite where the gay pride participants were observing. As floats for various gay social and political organizations passed, the protestors shouted through megaphones and held signs stating, "Got AIDS?," "God killed Sodom and Gomorrah," and "Die Fags." Things were surprisingly calm considering the atmosphere of conflict the protestors were inspiring. A few people went over to yell back, but for the most part, participants focused on the parade and did not give into the temptations of conflict. Watching the floats pass, we anxiously awaited the Green Country Two-Spirit Society float, which was one of the many gay organizations participating. When they passed, Sheila, in full jingle dance regalia, was sitting across the back of a Pendleton-blanket-covered red convertible Mercedes, waving as if she were homecoming queen. The car was followed by five other Two-Spirit men in their straight dance regalia, stepping to the blaring powwow music resonating from the car. Once the car and the dancers got close enough to hear, Jimmy and the other men standing in the street let out a celebratory "lululululu."[2] I watched for the expressions on people's faces and noticed some people were laughing, some people gazing like tourists at a powwow, and one person, baffled, asked his friend, "Are there gay Indians?"

The question of the existence of gay Indians came up multiple times during my fieldwork. While at dinner with a Cherokee family, some of the guests were inquisitive about my most recent research project. While I was telling them that I was working with a ceremonial and social subgroup of American Indians, the host interrupted, "They're gay, ya know, Two-Spirits, like berdache." The other guests, both Indian and non-Indian, looked surprised at this disclosure. A Cherokee man responded with many questions about Two-Spirit people and their history. As in most cases, the Indian people at the dinner had little to no idea about the respect once given to the gender different in historic Native societies. The conversation came to a close with his statement, "You would think that homosexuality wouldn't have spread into the Indian community."

I had known for some time from Two-Spirit people that the gay community did not recognize racial diversity, and especially not Natives. Also, I surmised that mainstream Native society did not react positively toward gay and lesbian Indians. I realized at that moment in the park that there were also no gay Indians according to gay society, and at the dinner I further understood that there were no gay Indians according to Native and mainstream society. What struck me most about this realization is the disjuncture that gay Indians cause in accepted signs and symbols of what American Indians are thought to represent. I brought this up later in the year during a discussion with Ben and Mick, two key men in Two-Spirit society:

— Brian: *People have asked me, "Are there gay Indians?"*
— Ben: *Yeah, that was like down at the gay pride, the protestors were saying, "Why are you all here?" . . . They couldn't believe it . . . ya know . . . and they thought we were degrading the Indian community by marching in a gay pride parade. See . . . people don't think . . . they have this thought in their mind . . .* warriors! *[laughs]*
— Mick: *Which we can be . . .*

— Ben: *Which we are . . . ya know, but we have different warrior types. I just love the way we are changing people's thinking about stereotypes.*

Given the identity politics surrounding being Native in the 21st century, contemporary Two-Spirit men are subject to accepted popular ideas, positive and negative, about what it means to be an American Indian. As Craig Womack (1999:280) points out, "I would speculate that a queer Indian presence fundamentally challenges the American mythos about Indians in a manner the public will not accept. . . . Further, identifying an Indian as lesbian or gay makes the Native radically resistant to the popular tendency to make Indians artifacts from the past, since no one associates such terms with the warrior days when men were men and buffalo were scared."

Inevitably, Two-Spirit identity is subject to the multiple cultural ideologies regulating Indianness, whiteness, gayness, straightness, masculinity, femininity, and authenticity. Emerging from the intersection of multiple influences is a Two-Spirit identity created and maintained in relation to dominant ideas about Indian and gay identity. Two-Spirit identity articulates with and manipulates ideologies of gay and Indian despite the failure of gay and lesbian culture to recognize Native Americans as an important aspect of their society, as well as other Indians' denial of Two-Spirit existence.

Gender Diversity and the Cultural Crossfire

Two-Spirit men are well aware that at one time in the history of Native America, mostly before European contact, sexual and gender diversity was an everyday aspect of life among most indigenous peoples. The following historical overview of Native American gender diversity is intended to help frame the ways contemporary Two-Spirit men are in the cultural crossfire between contemporary constructions of Native identity and historical knowledge. As we will see throughout the book, the history of acceptance of sexuality and gender diversity within Native communities places Two-Spirit men's desires at odds with contemporary community expectations.

What scholars generically refer to as "Native American gender diversity" was a fundamental institution among most tribal peoples. The fact that there were men among North America's tribal peoples who preferred to do women's work, dressed in a mixture of female and male clothing, and had sexual and domestic relationships with men is extensively documented in the academic and colonial-era literature.[3] However, among Native societies these male-bodied gender-different people, referred to as "berdaches" in the academic and colonial literature, were in fact not considered men; rather, they were a separate or third gender (Roscoe 1993:336–349).[4] Lang refers to the male-bodied third-gender person as women-men, which I find a convenient descriptive term in lieu of the colonial term berdache (1998:xvi). Not to be confused with transvestitism, this third gender often embodied a mixture of the social, ceremonial, and economic roles of men and women. For example, among the Zuni there were men, women, and *lhamana*. Lhamana was the third gender occupied by a male-bodied person. The lhamana dressed as women and performed women's crafts such as weaving and potting, but also had the physical strength to fulfill certain male-oriented pursuits such as hunting big game and cutting firewood (Roscoe 1991:22–28). Roscoe describes the Zuni lhamana We'wha who lived until 1896:

We'wha could not undergo the rites of passage specific to women because those depended on biological functions he did not possess. Even so, it is likely that he learned a certain amount of women's lore and ritual and joined female members of his household when they observed domestic rites. And since he did not give birth he was not subject to the taboos that required the periodic separation of the women from men. Thus, he could move freely in both male and female social worlds. The lhamana was, in functional terms, a nonwarrior or nonaggressive male, a crafts specialist rather than a primary producer, an individual who combined elements of male and female social, economic and religious roles. [1991:145]

Accordingly, historical Native ideas about gender did not employ the gender-binary, bodily-sex-equals-gender view commonly found in European society. Rather, male- and female-bodied persons had a myriad of gender roles that they fulfilled within their society. Genders as social categories of persons were a malleable part of an individual's identity and alterable throughout a person's lifetime (Lang 1998:59–66; Roscoe 1991:147–168, 195–198; 1993:338–341; 1998:6–16; Williams 1986:65–86).

As a separate category of persons, women-men went through a socialization process distinct to their gender role. In general, families and the people of a community observed children and noted their behavior before guiding them toward a particular form of gendered socialization. For example, if a young boy showed a tendency to "play war," his relatives would take notice and guide his education, as well as incorporate him socially and ritually in the direction of being a warrior. Young boys who showed a proclivity toward the work of women and same-sex desires were socialized into the role of the third gender. Women-men had specific rites of passage through which they passed before becoming a full member of their community. For example, Williams has noted that every child suspected to be a *winkte,* the Lakota male-bodied third gender, was taken to a ceremony to communicate with winkte ancestors in order to be reassured whether the child was going through "a phase" or whether his behavior was a "permanent" state of being (1986:54). If winkte status was confirmed during the ritual, then a child's path to becoming an adult, such as being taught to cook and sew, was determined. Another "test" was to give a child a choice between implements of work, such as a basket versus a bow (Whitehead 1993:504–505). For example, among the Northern Paiute, if the male child suspected of being a *tüvasa* chose the bow, then it was assumed that he was making a choice about his future gender socialization as a man, and if they took the female implements he would be socialized as the third gender (Lang 1998:236).[5] Being confirmed as a person who should be socialized as a third gender determined subsequent rites of passage as well as an individual's eventual status as an adult.

Because third-gender people were neither men nor women but their own gender, they were not bound by the same expectations and responsibilities. In most societies, women-men did not participate in the prestige system of hunting and war honors required of men. Women-men did not have to earn the respect of their people through acts of bravery,

9

because they gained their prestige through the obligation to the people that was built into their role. Just as men were expected to hunt and go to war, women-men were expected to help their extended families with domestic and ritual tasks and care for children. In addition, the role of the women-men was to make their specific talents available for the betterment of their society. Women-men were specialists whose work included taking on special roles in community rituals and producing specialized crafts (Lang 1998:151). For example, their gender-"neutral" status allowed them to cook ceremonial meals among peoples with menstrual taboos surrounding food preparation, such as the Navajo. Also, women-men were expected to perfect craft traditions. That is, women-men were given an opportunity to produce highly specialized forms of crafts, such as pottery or weavings, not intended for everyday use. Hastiin Klah, the well-known Navajo *nadleeh*, was recognized as a talented weaver of Navajo-style rugs. Klah learned weaving from his mother and sister and by his twenties was a well-known weaver among collectors of Native arts and crafts. During the increased influx of manufactured blankets and goods into Native society in the late 1800s, Klah single-handedly saved the art of Navajo weaving. Eventually, Klah and his weavings traveled to the World's Columbian Exposition in Chicago in 1893 (Roscoe 1998:47–48). Klah was unique in his public persona and the acceptance he was given by traders and collectors, no doubt because he chose to dress as a man instead of mixing gendered clothing. More importantly, Klah stands as an important example of the significance of the role of third-gender men in the maintenance of local culture.

Women-men's willingness to make sacrifices for the good of the society earned them a considerable amount of prestige and veneration. Women-men's difference was also seen as the design of the Creator (God) and therefore women-men were to be approached with reverence. Williams notes, "In a religion like the Lakotas', 'berdaches' [*winkte*] are seen as magical holders of unique ritual instructions. Since they are guided by a spirit, they are not bound by normal rules of conduct. This unusualness is an indication of their sacredness" (1986:32). The gender different were possessed of a special relationship with the

Creator because they were seen as being able to bridge the personal and spiritual gap between men and women. In this way they were to have come to the Creator with a "neutral heart." The neutrality of Cheyenne *hemaneh* made them sought out "go-betweens," providing services in courtship and marriage, such as bringing gifts from a suitor's family to that of the bride (Hoebel 1960:77; Schaeffer 1965:224). Among the Lakota, the naming of children to ensure they would grow up "without sickness" was a common role of the winkte (Hassrick 1964:122–123). Communities called upon the women-men to direct or take part in particular ceremonies because their gender ambivalence lacked the potentially dangerous extremes of men's virulence and women's reproductive capacity. Bowers notes the following about women-men among the Hidatsa:

Since the "berdaches" were viewed as mystic possessors of unique ritual instructions secured directly from the mysterious Holy Woman, they were treated as a special class of religious leaders. When the Sun Dance ceremonies were to be performed, it was the "berdaches" duty to locate the log for the central post. . . . The "berdaches" comprised the most active ceremonial class in the village. Their roles in ceremonies were many and exceeded those of the most distinguished tribal ceremonial leaders. [They were not] bound as firmly by traditional teachings coming down from the older generations through the ceremonies, but more as a result of their own individual and unique experiences with the supernatural. [1965:106–107]

Accordingly, the institution of the third gender was less about an individual's sexuality and more about the ways their special qualities were incorporated into the social and religious life of their community.

Evidence of important social roles has done little to quiet the controversy and speculation over the sexuality of women-men. It is well documented that women-men had sexual relations and domestic partnerships with other male-bodied persons designated by society as men. It is further assumed that women-men did not have sexual relations with other third-gendered men (Callender and Kochems 1983:449). Were women-men then "homosexual"? If we go by Western definitions of sexuality and bodily sex, then we could say that most were. Yet the fact remains that they were having sexual relations with people in different sex/gender categories than themselves. But I am also reluctant to call it heterosexuality, because third-gender people's sexuality or lifestyle was not heteronormative in the Western sense. There is evidence that the alternatively gendered also had sexual relations with both men and women, thereby being bisexual by contemporary Western definitions. However we wish to classify their sexuality and sexual behavior, the historical record supports, with little detail, that women-men had sexual relations with other male-bodied persons.[6]

It is misleading to examine women-men's sexuality outside its tribal cultural context, because women-men were sexually active within a multitude of social institutions. Furthermore, the scant information on exactly how women-men's sexuality was incorporated into tribal people's cultural ideology has led to significant speculation on the part of scholars. What is apparent, though, is that Native societies had an incredibly sophisticated way of viewing sexuality and how it fit into an individual's social identity. Women-men had a variety of sexual and partner relationships in the forms of marriages as well as short trysts with young single men and married men. Among the Mohaves, the *alyha* were courted by men and were considered wives upon marriage. Devereux interviewed one local Mohave leader who had multiple alyha wives and gave vivid descriptions of the ways they "imitated menstruation" and pregnancy. As full members of the man's household, the alyha wives had duties and responsibilities the same as the female-bodied wives but were more difficult to divorce because "they are so strong they might beat you up" (1937:511–514). Women-men also had occasional sexual encounters with married men who were following sex-avoidance taboos because their wife was either pregnant or menstruating. Also, women-men could provide a socially safe sexual alternative in Native societies where adultery was considered a significant social disruption and punished severely. Winktes were to have "taken visits" from young men who did not have socially acceptable outlets for sex, presumably because they lacked wealth or rank to be married. On other occasions men may have sought sex with a woman-man in an attempt to gather spiritual power or good luck in war. Women-men were also to have on occasion taken women as marriage and sexual partners (Lang 1998:206–207, 186–198; Williams 1986:100–101). Regardless of actual sex acts, what remains important to contemporary Two-Spirit men is that women-men's sexuality and gender difference were fully incorporated into tribal cultural ideologies.

Gender diversity, as with other Native cultural practices, however, had difficulty surviving amid the onslaught of Euro-American aggression. From the time of first contact with Europeans, gender diversity and same-sex relations were repressed by religious condemnation and violence. The Spanish were the most appalled by the acceptance of same-sex relations among the Native peoples they encountered. Indeed, "sodomy" and "transvestitism" among indigenous populations became a central reason to justify the conquest of North America. By contrasting Native licentiousness against their own virtuous Catholicism, the Spanish convinced themselves of the divine nature of their violence against Native peoples and the gender different. To Spanish cultural sensibilities, Indian susceptibility to European diseases was the rout of God against sodomites rather than a lack of immunity. In an often-quoted passage, Balboa "saw men dressed like women; [he] learned that they were sodomites and threw the king and forty others to be eaten by his dogs, a fine action of an honorable and Catholic Spaniard" (Roscoe 1991:172; Williams 1986:137).

Little is known about the fate of gender diversity between European conquest and the sparse mention of the institution in early anthropological accounts and the documents of Indian agents. Scholars assume tribal people reacted to Euro-American condemnation of the gender different by taking the practice underground and removing it from publicly held ceremonies. As Kroeber observed in 1940, "While the institution was in full bloom, the Caucasian attitude was one of repugnance and condemnation. This attitude quickly became communicated to the Indians and made subsequent personality inquiry difficult; the later berdaches [led] repressed or disguised lives" (1940:209). Roscoe points out that as the Spanish "engine of conquest" in New Mexico was slowed by changing attitudes within the Spanish government, they no longer needed moral justifications to dominate local Natives. Women-men were to have simply blended into the cultural landscape aided by the new Spanish indifference (1991:171–176).

However, we again find evidence of outside intervention in Native sexuality under the American bureaucratic system for dealing with and "assimilating" Indians on reservations. By 1883 the Indian agents overseeing Native populations on reservations and the Christian missionaries they supported were using the Code of Religious Offenses, or Religious Crimes Code, to aggressively attack Native sexual and marriage practices. The Code outlawed many of the ceremonial and public gatherings that Native people used to maintain their social and religious organization. The Code also attempted to restrict tribal practices of polygamy and pressure Natives to adopt Euro-American ideals of monogamy and lifelong marriage. Tribal peoples who did not abide by the Code were arrested and punished. Well into the late 1920s "Indians were jailed, penalized, and denied rations to enforce the Religious Crimes Code, while individual agents, far from Washington's supervision, often devised additional standards of their own" (Dozier 1958:446–447, 1964:97; Roscoe 1991:177).

In the 1890s the Crow *boté* Osh-Tisch became the target of the Crow reservation agent's disgust with the "debased standard of the people among whom he lives" (Roscoe 1998:35). Anthropologist Robert Lowie noted that "former agents have repeatedly tried to make him [Osh-Tisch] don male clothes, but the other Indians themselves protested against this saying it was against his nature" (1912:226). The agent was to have cut *botés'* hair, made them wear men's clothing, and force them into manual labor (Roscoe 1998:35; Williams 1986:179). Williams quotes a Crow consultant: "When the Baptist missionary Peltotz arrived in 1903, he condemned our traditions, including the *badé* [*boté*]. He told congregation members to stay away from Osh-Tisch and the other *badés*. He continued to condemn Osh-Tisch until his death in the late 1920s. That may be the reason why no others took up the *badé* role after Osh-Tisch died" (1986:183). Besides direct intervention with adults who were in women-men roles, children who might be third gender were swept up in the push to use education as a tool of assimilation in the boarding schools. Roscoe points out: "The environment in these schools was openly hostile to all forms of traditional Indian culture. 'Berdache' behaviors were quickly spotted and suppressed" (1991:199–200). Any women-men children who came to boarding school cross-dressed were made to wear men's clothes and join in men's work. In some cases women-men children were taken from boarding school to never be seen again, and winktes began killing themselves because they could not handle the pressures placed on them by government agencies and their changing communities (Williams 1986:181–183).

The change from public incorporation to the suppression of women-men's public roles is easily located in Native religious and cultural adaptations. As governmental efforts at assimilating Natives grew more intense, the gender different became an increasingly less visible part of the public culture of Native society, which occurred in tandem with the loss of ceremonial traditions and social practices in general. The result was a decline in the ceremonial use of women-men's roles and responsibilities. Once Indians began to convert to Christianity en masse, they also accepted ideologies about the sinfulness of same-sex relations. As a result, the history of gender diversity in Native North America has gone largely unnoticed by contemporary Native peoples. Those non-gay Indians who are aware of third-gender traditions mostly fail to make the connections between contemporary GLBT (gay, lesbian, bisexual, transgender) Natives and historic forms of sexuality and gender difference. At the same time, Two-Spirit men consistently look to the example set by historic women-men, whom they call *Two-Spirit ancestors*, for inspiration and guidance in the ways they conduct themselves and, more importantly, construct their identity.

Two Two-Spirit Societies

I witnessed the ways Two-Spirit men test the boundaries of Native and gay identities through the social relations of the Two-Spirit Society of Denver and the Green Country Two-Spirit Society. The Denver Society asked that I use their real name, whereas "Green Country Society" (GCS) is a moniker for a Two-Spirit organization in Oklahoma. The

Denver and Green Country societies are two examples of a trend in North America where GLBT Natives are becoming increasingly socially and politically organized. These organizations provide a safe place for GLBT men to socialize, get services such as counseling, and generally be themselves. Most men who participate in these organizations do so anonymously; therefore, at the request of GCS members all the names of the Two-Spirit men who are described or quoted in this book are fictitious. While most of the men will recognize themselves and one another, I sought to disguise them from the general public and from other Indians in their familial and tribal social circles.

The most recognizable individuals in the book are the men with whom I had the most contact and were the most forthcoming with information about their lives. They are also the men who were less worried about "being found out should some Indian put two and two together." One of the challenges in dealing with anonymity was addressing several people's desire to be named and dealing with the paralyzing fear that some men had about "being found out." Therefore, in order to protect the people who wished not to be identified, I reached a compromise with both parties by making certain people "known" without using their names, and disguising other people by attributing their comments to multiple fictitious people. Many of the people who are recognizable are public figures in the Two-Spirit and Native HIV/AIDS movement, and therefore easily recognizable to insiders.

Ben, Glen, Andy, and Sheila are disproportionately represented in this book. Ben and I became close friends over the five years that I worked with the GCS. Ben and I continue to stay in touch and are working on future projects on HIV/AIDS prevention among Natives. Because of my friendship with Ben and the frequency with which I spoke with him, he is quoted the most throughout the book. I also became close with Sheila, a Lakota man who has lived as a woman since her early teens. I originally came to know Sheila through the Denver Society. Sheila represents something special for Two-Spirit men. She is what many of the men consider the closest representation to the original women-men. Sheila's crossing of genders in dress was not necessarily what made her special, it was that she embodied all the things that had made the gender different special. Sheila is an extremely talented craftsperson and cook, and has extensive knowledge of ceremonial practices. The respect that people gave to Sheila and her words also accounts for the frequency with which she is quoted in the book. Glen is one of the leaders of the Denver Society and is very knowledgeable not only about Native customs but also about the history of gender diversity in Native America. While I never got to know Glen very well, I had many informative conversations with him and found him one of the most quotable men to interview. Andy was the one person who really scared me during my initial introduction. Andy is the founder of the Denver Society and is a zealous supporter of indigenous rights and Two-Spirit social and political goals. He is also a believer in Native ceremonialism in its most rigid contemporary forms. Andy's reputation for being combative and harsh preceded him, and I did come away from my initial meeting feeling like I had been interrogated. I eventually figured out that Andy shares the protectiveness of many Native people who have grown tired of outsiders' curiosity and exploitation. However, through interviewing Andy and spending some time with him, it became clear that his harshness was a reflection of his passion for the survival and well-being of Two-Spirit people. I became close friends with many Two-Spirit men, but most of them were wary of being identifiable in this book. Therefore, I have divided them into multiple people and made every effort to disguise details such as tribal identity and age.

Where are the women? The latter is a question about this book that I have had to answer multiple times. The absence of women in this book is more about the structure of the GCS, where I spent most of my time, and the Denver Society. The GCS is based out of a clinic that relies on grants for work with men who have sex with men, and therefore they are limited in the focus of their outreach and activities. The Denver Society is independent of any funding agency, but the group is divided along gender lines between male- and female-bodied persons, or between gays and lesbians. The men and women in the Denver Society will come together for larger events, but the men and women remain largely separated and engaged in their own social circles. This mirrors divisions in popular gay society between the social and political differ-ential situatedness of gay men and women. This separation made it dif-ficult to gain access to Two-Spirit women. Although I did interview and interact socially with Two-Spirit women, I did not accumulate enough information to fairly represent their interests or generalize about their identity in this book.

The reader will also notice a lack of focus on tribal identities. There are two reasons. First, this is a book about Two-Spirit men and the ways they deal with social alienation and self-acceptance. Therefore, it was important to privilege their voices rather than the voices of their tribes and potentially hostile non-gay Indians. Second, I am careful not to associate specific individuals with tribes out of an effort to disguise them. If I mention a tribe it is not the person's specific tribe, but one from the same culture area, with comparable social institutions and re-gional experience. This practice may obscure the importance of specific tribal interpretations of gender diversity and individual relationships with their tribes. However, on the whole, the people discussed and quoted in this book felt that their tribes were hostile to their sexuality and their gender differences.

The Journey to Cultural Compromise

This book is not only about gay Indians. It is also about the ways in which individuals find themselves as subjects of social processes and cultural ideology. I found that the effort given to becoming Two-Spirit, as a multitribal identity and a community, is on the one hand a reaction to the dominant Native ideologies that deny Two-Spirit men their place in tribal communities and Native culture at large. On the other hand, becoming Two-Spirit is also a path or journey that individuals travel to find something out about themselves in relation to their felt sense of racial, sexual, and gender identity. Most of the Two-Spirit men from the Denver Society and Green Country Society describe becoming Two-Spirit as a journey. It is a journey undertaken not only by individuals but by groups of people who together attempt to negotiate the rocky terrain of contemporary Native identity, tribal identity, and how to reconcile what they know non-gay Indians think about their sexuality and gender difference.

It would be redundant to point out that the path to becoming Two-Spirit is agentive, especially in light of scholarship that illustrates the ways people resist domination and alienation in small, everyday ways (Scott 1985, 1990). More importantly, though, the path to Two-Spiritedness is self-critical. Foucault tells us that individuals will come to know who they are in relation to dominant ideologies supported by systems of domination (1978, 1986, 1988, 1990). Therefore, individuals come to "know themselves" through repeated comparisons with the attributes reinforced by dominant ideology. For example, Two-Spirit men are aware that their sexuality and gender difference does not qualify as legitimately Indian within the dominant idea that all Indian men are straight and that contemporary Native society is heteronormative. Two-Spirit men come to know themselves as individuals who do not fit within the parameters of Indian identity as set out by their tribal communities, families, and Native society at large. Complementing Foucault, Butler shows us that the dominant ideologies that reinforce what "Indian" means rely on repetitive use within the social field. She further shows us that it is within this repetition that the potential for resistance resides (1990, 1992). Therefore, within the repeated comparisons that individuals make between dominant ideology and themselves are opportunities for variation on dominantly reinforced behaviors and ideas. That is, within the performance of Native social practices are opportunities to modify symbolic content to meet individual and group goals. The question that goes unanswered in Foucault's examination of domination and Butler's ideas of agency is, Where do individuals obtain the *desire* to reevaluate their position in the social structure and take critical action accordingly? Gramsci recognizes, as do Butler and Foucault, that domination is reliant on ideological assumptions (1971). The similarity between these three theorists allows us to observe how symbolic content is used in domination, and also how it is used to resist in tangible ways. By adding Gramsci's ideas about resistance, we can then examine how individuals are dominated by ideology, where openings for resistance occur, and more importantly, what leads to the critical redeployment of cultural ideas by subordinates.

Gramsci would call the signs and symbols used to regulate identity *common sense*. Common sense is the uncritically accepted ideas and assumptions held by a particular society, otherwise known as the dominant ideology. However, dominant ideology is not something fixed or immobile; rather, it is fluid and continuous in its absorption of ideas entering everyday life (Gramsci 1971:323–326). Critical action against dominant ideology does not transform common sense by brute force, but rather through the ongoing "war of position" based in that same ideology. Gramsci states that "it is not a question of introducing from scratch a scientific form of thought into everyone's individual life, but of renovating and making 'critical' an already existing activity" (1971:330–331). Therefore, the dominant discourse about the ideal or the "common sense" of ideal Indianness is challenged by Two-Spirit men, not by inventing a new form of Indianness, but rather by using existing signs from the social field in distinct and novel ways as a critique of limitations placed on Indian identity. That is, Two-Spirit men make use of multiple symbolic and social representations of their racial identity in compromise with multiple representations of their ideas about gender and sexuality. A "critical understanding of self" is instituted through the social struggle between ideas and discourses that operate to structure the political, practical, and theoretical aspects of individual awareness. This understanding becomes a means to action, whereby awareness of belonging to an individual and collective consciousness (here it is Two-Spirit) is realized in the practice and ideas associated with a particular social grouping (Gramsci 1971:333–335).

What I have termed *critical self-knowledge* is the dialectical relationship between constructions of self-knowledge, as it is influenced by the dominant ideology, and the critical assessment of a dominant ideology's relation to oneself. That is, critical self-knowledge is the process by which individuals construct a self-knowledge not by mere reflection, but by a critical awareness of the ways dominant ideology positions them. Individuals construct a self-knowledge, not by mere reflexivity against dominant ideal types of "Indianness" – albeit heteronormative – but by and through a critical awareness of how they are positioned by regulations on what qualifies as Indian according to dominant society. Resistance in the form of variation is then initiated by individual and collective critical awareness. Inevitably, cultural symbols are modified to this variation, for example, a Two-Spirit man dressing in female regalia at a powwow.

I draw on the idea of *cultural compromise* to explain the ways that Two-Spirit men critically engage the dominant ideologies that ensure their alienation while they also attempt to find a place for themselves within Native society and cultural ideology. A conceptual problem occurs when we see that individuals are critically aware of their alienation (critical self-knowledge) but at the same time wholeheartedly desire to be accepted by those people and societies that alienate them. That is, Two-Spirit men are largely opposed to the way that their communities treat them, yet they desperately want to be accepted as members of their communities without condition. They want their communities to not simply accept their sexuality and gender difference, but they want that difference to be reincorporated as it had been prior to Euro-American intervention. With this goal in mind, Two-Spirit men have become adept at finding conciliation between their desires to be full participants in their tribal communities, and their desire to alter the heterosexist ideologies that keep them away. In this way, the path to becoming Two-Spirit, and to agency, does not involve completely turning away from contemporary Native identity. Instead it involves bridging Two-Spirit sexuality and gender identity with Two-Spirit Native identity. Critical self-knowledge does not incite a complete reversal of dominant Native ideology, but rather it incites individuals to create a space within dominant ideology for themselves through slight variation. In this way, Two-Spirit men do not seek the wholesale change of contemporary Indian identity, but they want their gender diversity and sexuality to be accepted among the possible ways of being Indian. Therefore, the act of a man wearing a woman's buckskin dress and taking his performance seriously at a powwow is not simply a form of symbolic resistance, but is a process of reassociating the meaning of that symbol (the buckskin dress) with gender diversity. The form of women's buckskin dress and dance is not challenged; rather, it is only the available meanings for "buckskin dress" within the dominant ideology that are challenged. While Two-Spirit men free the women's buckskin dress and dance of its proprietary meaning, it remains true to the historic traditions that formed it and its contemporary associations with Indianness.

As we will see, Two-Spirit men work within the confines of Native American identity, only slightly modifying its heteronormative aspects, to create a space for themselves. In doing so, they seek a compromise between a culture that they cherish and their desire to be accepted.

CHAPTER TWO

From Gay to Indian

Most gay Indians in the 20th century found their refuge in closeted isolation on reservations and rural Native communities or in the non-Native-dominated world of the gay underground in cities. Some of the people in this book are in their late forties and early fifties, and they remember what it was like to be involved in a popular gay culture that paid little attention to their interests. Things changed for gay Natives in the 1980s when academics and activists began celebrating Native people's historic acceptance of sexuality and gender difference. Articles such as "The Bow and the Burden Strap" by Harriet Whitehead (1993) and the book *The Spirit and the Flesh* by Walter Williams (1986) became primers on indigenous gender diversity. The popular gay community began to embrace the idea of a tolerant Native society and readily used the berdache as a symbol to counter Western intolerance. In fact, multiple non-Native gay organizations included the word berdache in their titles. Unfortunately, the appropriation of the berdache did little to make gay and lesbian Natives any more comfortable in the gay community. Gay and lesbian Natives took back the symbol of gender diversity when in 1994 they began to refuse the colonial-derived term berdache and proposed the term Two-Spirit. This accomplished two things – it removed the negativity of colonial impressions of Native gender diversity and wrangled the concept away from the popular gay community. The result has been a successful but partial separation from popular gay society. More importantly, Two-Spirit has become an identity that Native gays and lesbians can adopt that does not rely on sexual orientation but instead finds its inspiration in Indian culture and society. However, the origins of Two-Spirit identity have a long history in a syncretism between gay and Native social practices that should be recognized before a full understanding of contemporary Two-Spirit identity can be reached.

— Rick: *It appears to me that the process of defining and maintaining our identities are not one way, but a continuing dialogue crossing distance and time. Many Two-Spirit people leave their community, for example their reservation, to find themselves in the larger picture of gay, lesbian, transgender people in this country. Initially it is liberating because of the freedom and opportunities afforded. It doesn't take too long to figure out Indians have little political power because of our small population. It doesn't take long to notice that the sense of community we are used to is simply not there [in gay society]. It is my experience that Indians ultimately assume an identity separate from the larger gay community. I am not sure that it is one fostered by racism within the gay community as much as our own sense of tribal identity.*

Indians and the Early Gay Movement

Throughout the latter half of the 20th century many gay and lesbian Natives moved to major cities seeking more tolerance than they experienced on reservations. With the fevered pitch of the post-Stonewall gay movement,[1] the social atmosphere of the 1970s was prime for the development of publicly active gay and lesbian organizations. Among the goals of gay and lesbian activism, as Altman points out, is to obtain civil rights as a minority (1979). At the heart of liberationist claims, gay activists pushed the notion of sexual orientation, characterized as a "fixed condition" at birth, which inevitably would bolster civil rights claims (d'Emilio 1992:3). While gay activists were seeking rights based on minority status, the gay civil rights movement was ignoring issues of concern for community members of color.

Despite the gay rights movement's claim of diversity, American Indians and other minorities saw themselves as explicitly left out of the movement, creating a perceptible difference between gay and lesbians of color and the larger gay community. In reaction to the racism of the white gay movement, early gay and lesbian Native organizations exerted a specific form of "identity deployment" as a calculated political and social action (Bernstein 1997). Identity deployment relied on shared Indian symbols and basic Indian community values as a public statement not only about being gay but also about being Indian. By emphasizing the differences between themselves and the gay community, gay and lesbian Native organizations drew attention to their specific needs. Gay and lesbian Indians recognized themselves as a double minority and saw their political activism as a way to become recognized in the gay community, as well as to fight the homophobia they experienced at Indian service organizations and communities (Roscoe 1998; Williams 1986).

As a result, in 1975, Gay American Indians (GAI), often recognized as the "first gay Indian organization" in the United States, was established in San Francisco to answer in part the lack of support for people of color in the gay and lesbian liberation struggle. Randy Burns, a Paiute, and Barbara Cameron, a Lakota, formed the organization through grassroots efforts, bringing together gay and lesbian Natives in the Bay Area to share a unified identity as gay and indigenous. Randy Burns talks about the beginning of GAI:

At the same time, we face oppression as gay people, too, sometimes within our own Indian communities. In 1975 when we were organizing GAI, the local American Indian center refused to post our flyers because they might "offend" people. When we participated in an American Indian Day held at a local university, we were told to take down our booth: "We don't want any trouble," they said. Back then, we expected to receive negative remarks, from not only the non-Indian community but from our Indian counterparts, as well. [1988:3]

Burns's efforts at organizing young gay and lesbian Natives represent the foundation of contemporary Two-Spirit society. More importantly, the hostility Burns encountered both among Indians and non-Indians led to the pattern of creating gay and lesbian Native organizations independent of the generic Native and gay communities. As we will see, this isolation is something that the individuals in this book attempted to overcome.

With the influx of more young gay Indians into San Francisco's highly visible gay community, activity among GAI grew, and by 1980 the organization had 150 members and by 1988 it had 1,000 members (Burns 1988:4; Roscoe 1998:98). Early on, GAI attempted to fulfill the role of existing Bay Area Indian social and service networks from which gay and lesbian Natives had previously been alienated. As Walter Williams states, "GAI members helped them get referrals for housing and jobs or student loans, and provided social opportunities in a mutual support group" (1986:211). With the emphasis on AIDS prevention in the late 1980s and early 1990s, GAI began to focus its efforts on the double oppression experienced by gay and lesbian Indians. Burns states: "As gay people, our health needs are not taken seriously by the government. As Indians, we often find that AIDS programs overlook important cultural differences and fail to reach many Indian people" (1988:4). With the establishment of the Indian AIDS Project and the American Indian AIDS Institute in the late 1980s and early 1990s, GAI was responsible for beginning the first education and training in HIV/AIDS prevention in the Bay Area indigenous community. The institutionalized homophobia and limited resources within the Indian Health Service led to many Native gays not receiving the treatment they needed to manage their HIV/AIDS or other ailments. With GAI's efforts, the Indian Center of All Nations (ICAN) was established in 1992 with the goal of providing services once denied to openly gay and lesbian Native Americans. The goal of ICAN was to provide medical and social services to people of all nations, and as spelled out in its bylaws, "all genders – that of 'Two-Spirits' as well as women and men" (Roscoe 1998:99–101).

With similar goals, American Indian Gays and Lesbians (AIGL) of Minneapolis was established in 1987 as a social group to connect local gay Natives with traditional values. AIGL also answered the call of the AIDS crisis by helping to establish the Minnesota American Indian AIDS Task Force and the National Indian AIDS Media Consortium. Other groups organized in major cities across North America include Gays and Lesbians of the First Nations in Toronto, We'wha and BarCheeAmpe in New York City, Nichiwakan in Winnipeg, Tahoma Two-Spirits of Seattle, Vancouver Two-Spirits, and Nations of the Four Directions in San Diego (Roscoe 1998:103–104). All these organizations had as their focus the social and personal connection of gay and lesbian Natives with traditional ways as well as the prevention of HIV/AIDS infection among American Indians. It is from these early organizations' efforts and inspiration that the national network of Two-Spirit societies was eventually founded.

Social Movement to Social Group

As the 1990s approached, the Native gay and lesbian community placed a greater emphasis on the indigenous gay experience versus that of popular gay society. Undeniably, the indigenous gay experience was one that intersected with racial politics in America, and that inevitably engaged issues of individual racial identity. Armed with the knowledge that gender-different persons historically were respected in their communities, indigenous gays began to emphasize their cultural heritage through the establishment of Two-Spirit as a kind of personhood and as a socially observable fact. Although early gay and lesbian Native organizations such as GAI were providing some of the same support-group services as Two-Spirit societies, Two-Spirit became a social identity with which large numbers of individuals across North America could identify. As a result of the movement away from specifically gay-community-oriented organizations, Two-Spirit societies began to emerge in the early 1990s. The move toward Two-Spirit societies and the use of the term Two-Spirit instead of the now gay-community-appropriated berdache signaled a transformation in the ways in which Native gays and lesbians saw themselves (Roscoe 1998; Thomas and Jacobs 1999). This transition also began a separation from the gay community that many Two-Spirit persons saw as necessary for the political and social maturity of indigenous gay communities.

By the early 1990s the mass political action of the gay community of the late 1980s was eventually overwhelmed by "racial reactions" (Edwards 2000:487). It is no coincidence that the beginning of the 1990s saw a surge in isolationist interest groups of gay women and men of color who saw themselves as underrepresented in gay activist goals. Edwards states: "Others, including most women and people of color, argued that treatment activism included challenging the racism and sexism of the medical research establishment. . . . To them 'fighting AIDS' also meant securing access to basic health care, treatment for drug addiction . . . [as well as] culturally specific AIDS education, and the condoms and clean needles required to reduce the risks of HIV transmission" (2000:495). The emphasis of support groups built around Two-Spiritedness is in part the Indian answer for providing culturally specific service and culturally specific experiences of gayness. As Albert McLeod assessed in his report from the 11th Annual International Two-Spirit Gathering: "The presences of a broader indigenous gay and lesbian community and network seems to correlate with the growing AIDS epidemic in the United States and Canada. While AIDS was devastating the gay community, HIV prevention campaigns began to create more awareness and discussion of sexuality, orientation and diversity. This openness may have been one of the influences that galvanized urban indigenous gays and lesbians to begin to identify and address issues that affected them like racism, substance abuse, homophobia, spirituality, and identity" (1998:1).

The increasing popularity of the term Two-Spirit as a way to describe the unique position of gay and lesbian Indians resulted in the establishment of more and more Two-Spirit communities. Given the flexibility of the concept of Two-Spirit, more people felt a greater connection to their Indian identity previously unavailable to them because of issues of blood quantum, tribal enrollment, and physical appearance. Two-Spirit had the unique ability to be "deployed as a panhistorical as well as a pantribal term" and concept (Roscoe 1998:111). As a result, many organizations began changing their names – removing the terms gay and Indian and including the term Two-Spirit – as a way to promote inclusivity. Urban gay Indians began to experience an alternative social realm to the gay white community and were also able to identify themselves and socialize in ways not previously recognized as possible.

Two-Spirit society, as it was represented not only by political/social organizations but also by a set of social relations, emerged as an alternative to the bar-based gay culture, and became a space where individuals not only could feel comfortable with being gay but also could reassociate themselves with their Indian identity. Many of the people in this book expressed dismay at the predicament of being Indian and participating in a popular gay culture associated with alcohol abuse and racism. It is no secret that popular gay culture is based in a bar social scene markedly separate from non-gay social spheres. Usually, the first place gay people go to "find others like them" in a new city or region is the local gay bar or dance club. Gay bar culture, combined with the negative impact of alcohol on the Native population, creates a difficult position for gay and lesbian Natives. As Phillip, a Two-Spirit Apache, told me, "If you want to find sex, meet other gay people, and feel free to behave how you want, there is no other place for people to go except gay bars." He went on to talk about the problem of being Indian in this atmosphere: "Whatever gay is, it isn't Indian and everything gay is new, young, thin, white, wasted, and sexy. When I go to these places I feel conspicuous because I am obviously Indian. I don't get as many negative responses since people know me from drag shows, but other people I know really would rather not be Indian and just gay so they can have fun." He further explained that the connections established between Two-Spirit people as a result of the creation of a specifically Two-Spirit space provided him with an escape from the "gay" atmosphere and opportunity for friendships and relationships with people who shared his same values and heritage. However, he also felt that the Two-Spirit society could be more limiting in options for friends and partners than the popular gay scene because so many Indians would not participate in Two-Spirit society. Important about Phillip's and others' feelings is the recognition of the alternative that Two-Spirit society offers individuals to be social, find partners and friends, and most importantly to many, be Indian.

At the same time that the gay community is perceived as having overwhelming negative aspects, Two-Spirit societies are not completely disassociated with the gay community, as they participate in gay pride parades, marches, and the bar scene. As we will see later, many Two-Spirit people, including the Denver and Oklahoma groups as a whole, used gay community events and gathering places as avenues to create awareness and to recruit new members. Furthermore, as the number of gay and lesbian American Indians participating in Two-Spirit social groups is limited, many people participated in the dating and social activities of the larger gay community and bar scene to expand their choices in sexual partners and friendships.

From Term to Identity

The transition from being a "gay Indian" to "Two-Spirit" and the establishment of Two-Spirit societies created an alternative identity for many of the largely urban-oriented indigenous gay and lesbian people. However, the term Two-Spirit had another effect: it allowed individuals who were still living within the cultural and social sphere of their tribal communities a way of bringing together their sexual orientation and their Native identity. When we consider that only a handful of Native communities continue to have words for gender-different people in their language, and still fewer have social roles for alternative genders, we can see the benefit of Two-Spirit as a descriptive term and concept. This flexibility is in large part responsible for the seemingly overnight acceptance and use of the term by Native gays and lesbians. Also, giving a Native-oriented name to one's identity takes one's sexual orientation out of association with "white" ways and places it within the realm of Indian culture. However, something occurred that I think surprised the gay and lesbian Natives who proposed the term Two-Spirit in the 1990s: use of the term moved from being a point of social and political solidarity to also becoming an *identity*. For most of the men in this book, Two-Spirit is an identity that is used the same way they might use their tribal affiliation to say something about their cultural heritage. Scholarly debate on what Two-Spirit means has tended to shy away from the idea of Two-Spirit as an identity; instead, it emphasizes the use of Two-Spirit as a social and political moniker.

Many academics present the term Two-Spirit as a "pan-Indian" social movement (Epple 1998; Goulet 1996; Lang 1998; Roscoe 1993, 1998). However, the Two-Spirit men represented in this book repeatedly saw themselves as distinct products of particular tribal traditions and used Two-Spirit as an identity through which to work for their acceptance within tribal communities. Pan-Indianism implies that the individuals who might use Two-Spirit as an identity have lost their cultural distinctiveness through the invention of a supratribal consciousness.[2] Jackson makes a point worth considering: "Pan-Indianism assumes that individuals or groups engaging in social gatherings across tribal or national boundaries will increasingly lose their cultural distinctiveness ... but it also ignores the capacity of communities to consciously maintain distinctive local practices in interactionally complex settings" (2000:45). Accordingly, scholars of North American gender diversity would have us believe that Two-Spirit is more suited for individuals who have no connection with their tribal identities through personal relationships or geography (Epple 1998; Goulet 1996; Lang 1998; Thomas and Jacobs 1999). Two-Spirit is intended to be a multitribal identity; however, it is also used to reference a tradition that is no longer publicly acknowledged in Indian communities. We must keep in mind that most Indian communities in North America no longer have social roles for multiple genders. I was often reminded that the decline in public roles paralleled the decline in Native language use, and as a result, the words for multiple genders are no longer part of the public discourse. Often people would refer to themselves and others as a Two-Spirit person affiliated with a particular tribal tradition, such as a "Seminole Two-Spirit."

Instead of conceptualizing Two-Spirit identity and organizations as a pan-Indian phenomenon, Two-Spirit men see their identities as continuations and extensions of social roles and identities within Native communities. Two-Spirit subjective experience occurs through the convexities of modern Indian and gay experience, while being acutely aware of historically rigid discourses within tribal and multitribal Indian communities. In this sense, Two-Spirit creative aesthetics and social practice do the work of identity through the destabilization of contemporary Indian discourse and the discovery of tradition, tribal or otherwise. That is, the performance of things Two-Spirit – holding ceremonies, mastering crafts, dancing, structuring social relations – proffer authentic proof of a Two-Spirit trans-temporal and trans-spatial relationship with tribal social customs.

As we will see, it is in the context of learning specific tribal traditions and the ceremonial and cultural preservation aspects of Two-Spiritedness where identity is formed and modified as a specific representation of Indian. Practices such as sweat lodges, beading, regalia making, healing ceremonies, and blessing newlyweds represent just a few ways I observed Two-Spirit people connecting with traditions of gender diversity and individual tribal identity. Two-Spirit society is not only a set of social relationships, but it also provides access to the cultural practices and ideals for the development of one's identity as Two-Spirit. In this way, Two-Spirit identity and cultural practice becomes one aspect of the fluidity of individual identity, where people emphasize their connectedness with the broader notion of Indian and Two-Spirit as well as highly specific identities associated with tribe or ceremonial communities.

The Scope of Two-Spirit Social Relations

During the course of my time with the Oklahoma and Denver groups, I observed the Two-Spirit society emerging as the quintessential social relation for many indigenous gays. There are numerous Two-Spirit organizations across America and Canada, and many of them, such as the San Francisco, Minneapolis, and Winnipeg groups, have existed for more than ten years. However, emerging more recently are organizations in smaller cities, as well as rural and reservation areas, that tailor their activities to the specific needs of group members in order to emphasize a spiritual and cultural connection to their Native identity. Societies represent a formalization of relationships between people who identify as Two-Spirit, but also, as Phillip reminded me, "They give us what we need. What we are not getting from our own tribes and families." Accordingly, it is through and by these societies that many people make the connections needed to "feel Indian."

Sean echoed this: "To me, my journey is to get in touch with my Native Americanness . . . the Native American side of me. It's something that I feel that connects me with the big picture. My generation is lost . . . our generation doesn't have a connection to our culture and I feel that I need to feel connected. Being Two-Spirit is being connected to that specific part of me." Being connected to Indian culture was one of the primary reasons that individuals gave for participating in Two-Spirit organizations and social activities. For many, Two-Spirit society represented a space where one could comfortably identify as being Indian without enduring the fear of homophobic reactions from other Natives. Two-Spirit society also provided a space where individuals who were alienated from participation in their tribal community could perceive themselves as playing a significant role in an aspect of Indian society. Activities such as gatherings, group participation in powwows, group meetings, and generally hanging out at people's houses doing beadwork or socializing, all acted to provide the needed social interaction and connection to "Indianness" that so many were seeking.

The Green Country Two-Spirit Society

The Green Country Two-Spirit Society was born out of the emerging concern for the spread of HIV/AIDS among communities of color in Oklahoma. In the early 1990s the Indian Clinic in the city of Eagleton, Oklahoma, responded to the increase of HIV/AIDS infection among gay Indian men by creating a department devoted solely to HIV/AIDS education, testing, counseling, and intervention. Part of the clinic's outreach program included a support group for gay Indian men. Within the outreach prevention materials and presentations was information about the history of Native American gender diversity and the new term Two-Spirit. Not only did the prevention outreach increase knowledge about HIV, but it also introduced Native men to the idea that their sexuality was once an accepted aspect of Native society. As a result, Native men in Oklahoma were becoming more aware of the gay indigenous movement and new literature on the concept of Two-Spirit. The idea of Two-Spiritedness also created a point of solidarity around which they could organize. For the members of the Eagleton group, Two-Spirit society was unlike other gay organizations that focused on political issues or fetishes. Rather, it was a group that made their sexuality a central aspect of their experiences as men of Native ancestry. The popularity of the Eagleton Society was in large part due to its ability to bring these two experiences together in a positive way. By the time of my involvement with the GCS in 1998, the small support group had developed into a full-fledged multitribal Indian community.

The men's reasons for participating in the GCS were as varied as their backgrounds. For many it was simply to be around other gay Indians who were sympathetic to their experiences, while some men used the society as an escape from their closeted life. Throughout my time with the GCS, I saw multiple men move in and out of the group, some returning after a short time away, while others seemed to disappear altogether. The core social activity for the men was the bimonthly group meetings at the clinic. These meetings usually involved a meal or snacks and lots of conversation. In many ways the activities at the bimonthly meetings were inconsequential to participants. Whether the meetings were spent beading, singing, hanging around, or taking part in a safe-sex workshop, it was the camaraderie that kept the men engaged. Ben saw the group as a starting point for the men to begin their journey to self-acceptance, a place to build confidence about their sexual orientation and racial identity. Once the men began to be comfortable with their identity, they would be more comfortable in other social settings. Ben saw this confidence as allowing the men to "no longer hide out in gay society," but to be Two-Spirit and participate in their Native communities "with pride and self-respect." In this way the group served its purpose as a social home base for the men, whose social lives involved alternating participation in tribal and urban Indian communities, families, and the gay community, all of which involved varying degrees of comfort and anxiety.

Outside the GCS the men's attentions are somewhat divided into two social orientations: those who participate more in Indian cultural activities and those who participate more in the gay community. Two-Spirit participation in the Indian community is largely determined by some kind of familial or social tie to tribal culture or individual and familial ties to the powwow community. Ben was the driving influence for participation of Two-Spirit men in local Indian culture. Although some GCS members had extensive experience in their tribal community, Ben's involvement in ceremonies, powwows, and the local Indian church provided an entrée to Native social circles for many GCS members. People who accompanied Ben to powwows or ceremonies would have been reluctant to participate without Ben's guidance. Breaking into Native social circles can be difficult in Oklahoma, and Ben's ease with his own identity provided the confidence they needed to feel comfortable in Native social situations. However, most of the men involved in their tribe's culture attempted to keep their Two-Spirit identity secret, or at least out of the forefront of their identity, in the tribal context. Many of the men only participated in Two-Spirit meetings and local powwows largely because of the anonymity provided by larger social events. To participate in tribal events where they were known, such as ceremonies and festivals, generated more anxiety about meeting the disapproval of other Indians.

Often, however, feelings of alienation from Native society pushed many people toward the gay community. Connections to non-gay Indians were tenuous for some, but most had extensive experience with the gay community. The gay community, particularly the urban bar scene, provided the anonymity not available in Indian communities. Eagleton has five or six known gay bars where the clientele is largely divided along class and age lines. Some bars are known as "troll" bars – a gay phrase indicating a place where unattractive, older, and largely working-class men hang out. Other bars had reputations for drawing younger professional crowds and "party boys," who are young unattached men first exploring the gay scene. In most cities the gay bar scene is also divided according to taste in music and culture, such as country and western gay bars or techno dance music bars. The GCS members who go to bars have their favorite hangouts where they often have established social circles independent of their Indian identity. It is important to remember that part of one's identity as Two-Spirit is sexual orientation, and the demand for lovers and partners inevitably draws men to the gay community. I saw several of the men intensify their participation in the gay community at the expense of the Green Country Two-Spirit community for a number of reasons, such as non-Indian partners, disagreements with other group members, or simply the pull of the sexually charged gay lifestyle.

The social participation of the GCS existed along an urban-rural continuum. That is, about half the men and most of the men's tribal communities and families lived in highly populated Indian rural areas. The Native population of Oklahoma, in general, is concentrated in former reservation areas.[3] As a result, there are large, tribally specific populations concentrated around small cities, such as Holdenville, which is mostly populated by Mvskoke peoples. These tribally specific geographic areas serve Oklahoma Indians as a cultural home in the same way that a reservation might. In and around these Indian towns are tribal government centers, ceremonial grounds, and tribal bingo parlors. A good number of the GCS men lived in tribally specific towns and would make the one- to one-and-a-half-hour drive to Eagleton for the weekly meetings. Frequently, they would also travel to Eagleton for weekend trips, staying with GCS members living in Eagleton and going out to gay bars. Because of the thriving gay scene, many of the rural men saw Eagleton and the Two-Spirit society as a place of freedom where they could avoid the watchful and potentially harmful gaze of other Indians. The men who lived closer to their tribal communities and families did have greater opportunities for participation in Indian cultural events, albeit "closeted" participation.

The urban nature of Eagleton provided a more open lifestyle in terms of sexuality, but the men remained cautious about their orientation around the tightly knit urban Indian community. Because Eagleton is so close to major tribal populations, it has a fairly concentrated Native population that is very active in an Indian Christian church and the powwow scene. Many of the GCS men had relatives or friends of the family, whom they were not "out" to, who were also involved in the urban community. As a result, they shared a similar predicament to the more rural men. However, the multitribal nature and large size of events such as powwows often allowed the men to blend in with their surroundings. Men living in Eagleton would leave the safety of the city, traveling to rural areas to see their families or participate in tribal community activities. The close proximity of their communities allowed them to spend enough time there to maintain social relations but avoid long-term scrutiny by relatives. The men maintained a con-

38

tinual balancing act between meeting community expectations for participation and guarding their "secret."

The Two-Spirit Society of Denver

The social experiences of the Denver group members as both Native and gay are distinctly urban. Denver has both a thriving Indian community and gay community, which are both large enough and diverse enough to provide varied degrees of participation. Unlike the GCS members, most Denver men lived great distances from their families and tribal homelands and reservations. This lack of access accounts for the central role the society played in the men's spirituality and social lives. Those men who grew up in metropolitan areas – "city Indians" as people called them – were more familiar with powwow culture than they were with ceremonial culture. People who had moved to Denver from a reservation or Indian community often brought with them knowledge of tribal culture, but seemed turned off by the ways of urban Indians. Regardless of their upbringing, the Two-Spirit society was the only connection to Indianness for many of the men. As the Green Country Society served as an escape from one's tribal community, the Denver group developed out of the need for a social and spiritual community.

While the Oklahoma group is supported by the Indian bureaucracy, the Denver group is solely self-sustaining, using HIV program money, prevention outreach grants, and personal funds to sponsor much of their travel, meeting, and gathering needs. The Two-Spirit Society of Denver was organized following a vision that Andy had after attending the International Two-Spirit Gathering in the late 1990s. Having experienced the positive atmosphere of the gathering, Andy was called to organize a Two-Spirit society that addressed many of the problems faced by gay and lesbian Indians in the Denver area. He felt that Indian gay men in particular lived self-destructive lives largely influenced by the vices of gay culture. Andy also felt that he and other Native men had been alienated from the spiritual benefits of participation in their communities. Andy's vision of a Two-Spirit society not only involved socializing but emphasized the ceremonial practices missing from urban Two-Spirit people's lives. By the time Andy began to organize indigenous lesbigays in the Denver area, the term Two-Spirit had become widely used in the gay Indian community and in publications such as *Two-Spirit People*, a collection of essays on Native gender diversity (Jacobs et al. 1997). Books such as this became primers for the movement in their emphasis on self-acceptance, common experience, community responsibility, and, most importantly for Andy, spirituality. Andy's intensity about the spiritual role of Two-Spirit people was at times at odds with the men who were seeking a form of fellowship with other Indian men. These two orientations somewhat divided the Denver group into three crosscutting interest groups: those who primarily saw the society as a spiritual outlet, those who saw the society as something more social, and the few people who participated in both the spiritual and social aspects of group activities.

Most of the activities that Andy organized were for spiritual purposes, such as sweats, practicing Sun Dance songs, and ceremonial instruction. By emphasizing Native spirituality, Andy sought to give gay and lesbian Natives access to spirituality without invoking the negative experiences that many GLBT Indians have with Christian churches and tribal communities. In my conversations with Andy, he consistently emphasized the spiritual aspect of Two-Spirit identity as the way to inspire indigenous gays and lesbians to live a healthy life, which includes having positive social and romantic relationships, resisting substance abuse, having self-respect, and practicing safe sex. Andy was resolute about Two-Spiritedness as a way of life focused on prayer, ceremony, and service to Indian people. Although Andy was welcoming to newcomers with little knowledge, he expected people to have a significant commitment to learning ceremonial practices. His approach could be alienating to Two-Spirits who did not grow up in traditional families or communities. Sheila and Glen helped temper Andy's intensity with their mild manner and Indian humor. However, ceremonial activities required a reverence that many people found uncomfortable, and participation in that aspect of the society fluctuated except for a committed core group. Andy organized some form of ceremonially oriented activity at least once a week, such as practicing Sun Dance songs, sweat lodges, and smaller ceremonies to help group members who were in need of spiritual guidance.

Ceremonies were important to the men, but social activities provided the foundation of the group. Sheila and Glen, while also committed to spirituality, were often responsible for the nonceremonial aspect of group activities, which included cookouts, teaching crafts, outings to bars, organizing the float for the gay pride parade, trips to powwows, and generally hanging out. Glen and Pete's high-rise apartment in the middle of the Denver gay district was the central gathering place for social activities and the launching pad for nights out in the gay bars. When in Denver I often stayed at Glen and Pete's amid the coming and going of group members stopping by to say hello, getting advice on craft projects, ad hoc singing, and just hanging around telling funny stories. I spent several Saturdays parked on Glen's couch listening attentively to gossip about boys, plans for new regalia, and local gay and Indian politics. Chuck's, a western gay bar, was the favorite hangout of the Denver Society. On Friday and Saturday nights a group of Indian men would accumulate in the back corner and spend the evening telling stories about sexual conquests, assessing the "scenery," and telling jokes.

Participation in popular Indian and gay culture, such as powwows and political marches, was also an important part of the Denver men's lives. In addition to Andy's commitment to organizing Two-Spirit ceremonies, he also organized people around indigenous political issues. He was an instrumental part of the local anti–Columbus Day activities and helped with marches and fundraising for indigenous issues in Central and Latin America. When Fred Martinez Jr. was murdered in 2001 in a gay-bashing incident, Andy, Sheila, and Glen organized a vigil and silent protest to the treatment of gays. By holding fundraisers in gay bars, having a float in the gay pride parade, and conducting outreach at gay community events, the group is also a highly visible part of the larger gay community in Denver. The Denver Society was far more publicly involved as a group than the Green Country Society was, no doubt because of the anonymity that the city provided.

The Denver men, however, drew less attention to issues of sexuality and gender when dealing with the local Indian community. Most of the core members of the Denver group danced in local powwows, and some participated in local ceremonial communities. Sheila and Glen often organized outings to powwows in the Denver area as well as trips to powwows in New Mexico and Oklahoma. During these events the men made more of an effort to blend into the crowd of participants and were mainly focused on their dance performances and on enjoying the powwow. At the same time, most of the people who went to powwows were "comfortably queer," a phrase I heard used occasionally. Comfortably queer simply meant that they were involved in Indian social circles and did not go to great lengths to hide their gender difference or sexuality, nor were they going to make it an issue of notoriety. Later in the book, we will see that non-gay Indians were at times openly hostile to Two-Spirit men despite their attempts to remain anonymous. Andy was also highly involved with a local ceremonial community surrounding a Lakota medicine person. At a Luwampi, commonly known as a "house ceremony," that I attended with Glen and Sheila, Andy took a major role in helping the medicine man set up the altar, and later he was in charge of accumulating the flesh offerings and placing them in tobacco ties. Andy did not wear any special clothing or take on any special role (that I was made aware of) associated with the gender different. Andy told me that he was fully out to the medicine person and most of the people who attended the ceremony, and that "no one really cared, because I was there for the patients and the people in the community." However, he did say that he would like to take on roles in ceremonies that were historically prescribed for the gender different. For the most part, the Denver men enjoyed a freedom that the GCS men were less reluctant to explore within their tribal communities. This difference inevitably influences the perspective on what being Two-Spirit means, and how the men go about being Two-Spirit.

Gathering

One afternoon at the Oklahoma annual gathering, Andy told me that he saw such events as historical memory in the making. He went on to explain that he imagined Two-Spirit people gathered in the same way as they were at that moment before the arrival of Europeans. The Two-Spirit people, traveling with their bands or tribes, would congregate with one another away from the main camp and socialize in a way that only Two-Spirits "would understand." At these historic gatherings Two-Spirit people would have taken part in some of the same activities as contemporary Two-Spirits, such as learning crafts, ceremonial ways, and the rejuvenation of their identity. Important in Andy's discussion is the assumption that Two-Spirit people through time have shared the differences and similarities currently manifested in their social relations, including the use of the gathering to support the Two-Spirit way.

Gatherings are social events, usually held over spring and summer weekends, where people come from all over North America at the invitation of another Two-Spirit society. Most gatherings follow a basic format of socializing, some cultural events such as talking circles, and a small powwow, while others incorporate more ceremonial practices such as sweat lodges. HIV/AIDS funding from Indian health agencies and AIDS prevention grants are often used to sponsor such gatherings; therefore, all tend to have workshops, talks, or sweats that deal specifically with these issues. Due to the negative impact of alcohol on the Native community, all the retreats are alcohol- and drug-free, and often incorporate substance abuse workshops as an aspect of the gathering. Also, workshops emphasize the building of self-esteem and healthy long-term relationships with partners through such Indian-specific therapeutics as talking circles and sweats.

Gatherings have their origin in the first open and public gathering of gay and lesbian Natives, called "The Basket and the Bow: A Gathering of Lesbian and Gay Native Americans," hosted by the American Indian Gays and Lesbians (AIGL) of Minneapolis at the Minneapolis American Indian Center during the summer of 1988. As McLeod explains: "The name for the gathering was derived from a Shoshone-Bannock tradition, which allows children to choose their sexuality, symbolized by either a basket or a bow" (1998:3). Over 60 participants from across North America attended the gathering. At the first gathering they held a woman's pipe ceremony, talking circles, giveaway, and workshops on AIDS, coming out, relationships, and chemical dependency (Roscoe

1998:109). The positive impact of this gathering spread rapidly and developed into what is now recognized as the "International Two-Spirit Gathering." The International Gathering attempts to bring together gay and lesbian First Nations and Indian peoples from all over North America for unity in social, ceremonial, and political practice and has been held every year since 1988, with the location alternating between Canada and the United States.

Gatherings among Two-Spirit groups nationwide have assumed two forms, those that are primarily spiritual and those that are mostly social. Overall, there are more social-type gatherings held annually than there are spiritual ones. Each gathering serves a different purpose and holds a different meaning for each Two-Spirit person. Despite the differences in focus, both gatherings have the same goal: to help Native gays and lesbians come to respect themselves as both gay and indigenous. The spiritual gathering accomplishes this by focusing on the historic and contemporary importance of Two-Spirit people's role in Native ceremonial contexts. The ceremonial gathering gives Two-Spirit people access to ceremonial contexts, contact with elders, and instruction in Native cultural practices. The social gathering can serve the same purpose, but it provides a more emotionally relaxed environment where cultural aspects of both Native and mainstream gay societies are also expressed.

Gatherings are probably the single most important feature of the Two-Spirit social world in that they represent one of the few places where Two-Spirit people feel comfortable being both Indian and gay. Gatherings help resolve the seemingly inherent conflict between gay and Indian social worlds. The events such as drag shows, powwows, hand games, and HIV/AIDS workshops combine the cultural worlds of Indian and gay. This syncretism allows for men to modify both cultures to fit their needs in the absence of the historic ideology that accepted gender difference in Native society. By bringing together gay and Indian social worlds, Two-Spirit people are making sex and gender difference a part of public Indian identity. No other Indian social context provides this opportunity. There is no other place where Two-Spirit men can dance in women's regalia at a powwow, take on female ceremonial roles, and mix gender roles in tasks around camps. Even more simple things such as holding hands with one's partner, openly flirting with someone of your same sex, and behaving femininely are all freedoms not afforded in other Indian social contexts. As Ben said, "The gathering is so popular because of the balance between Native and gay cultural practices. Some of these queens have never been around traditional activities and we can't shove it down their throat. We are also here to have fun and to show people how to be healthy Two-Spirits."

Gatherings also provide the social relations important to community and identity maintenance. Just as any Native cultural event is designed to bring people together and promote good feelings about one's identity, the Two-Spirit gathering emphasizes solidarity among Two-Spirit people regardless of tribal affiliation. It is not uncommon for regional gatherings, such as those of the GCS and Denver Society, to draw 50 to 60 people of multiple tribal backgrounds who have traveled over a thousand miles. At the gatherings, people meet other people with whom they share the similar experience of being gay and Indian, but they also participate in the shaping of what it means to be Two-Spirit. Andy and others often used the Lakota term *mitakuye oyasin* [We are all related] in reference to Two-Spirit people. Gatherings reflect this idea because it is there that connections are made between societies and individuals that last for years.

In July of 2000 I made the ten-hour drive along with Robert from Oklahoma to the secluded Wenakuo mountain camp just northeast of Denver. After parking our car, we made a one-mile hike with our gear to the isolated campsite. As we approached the camp we could see a couple of tipis through the trees and smell smoke from the fires. As we got closer we could hear the choruses of laughter that usually accompanied any Two-Spirit event. When we entered the camp we received the usual long line of embraces from our friends and "brothers." We were immediately escorted to the ceremonial fire where we were smoked off with sage and cedar. Some people were making breakfast and others were preparing the lodge for the morning sweat. Looking at all this activity, I was amazed at the sheer number of people who had endured camping without toilets or running water, and had been eating camp food for the previous ten days. For those ten days, around 60 people from all over North America had been going to lodge daily, cooking meals, gathering firewood, holding meetings, teaching crafts, and participating in ceremonies, and two people had "gone up on the hill" for vision quests. During the giveaway on the last day of camp, one person was made a pipe carrier, and many others were given their first eagle feather. Many times I had heard about how physically and emotionally draining the Wenakuo could be, but the commitment to learn and experience Indian ways on the part of people attending was overwhelming. When I pointed this out to Jeff, he glowingly said, "I just wish the elders could be here to see it."

After the establishment of the Denver group, Andy and several other socially and politically active Two-Spirits organized the Wenakuo "welcome home" retreat in 1997 to fulfill the traditional spiritual needs of Two-Spirit people. As Andy and Sheila explained it, the Wenakuo attempts to teach and emphasize responsibility to oneself, one's community, and one's spirituality. Wenakuo is the place where Two-Spirit people go to learn not only contemporary Indian cultural ways but their traditional roles, especially for those who were not raised "traditional." Elders and specialists teach how to conduct ceremonies and vision quests, ways of communicating with spirits, powwow drumming, and how to make regalia. Andy sees his role in helping organize the Wenakuo as a way to teach Two-Spirit people how to fulfill their role and send them out into the community to do "good work" with Two-Spirit and non-Two-Spirit Indian communities. As we will see in the following chapters, the Wenakuo represents the place where many individuals' journeys begin or are invigorated through the use of established and appropriated cultural traditions.

Unlike the Oklahoma gathering, the Wenakuo specifically prohibits non-Native gays from attending, sex between participants or couples is not allowed, everyone must do some form of cooking, gathering wood, or cleaning, and most everyone is expected to participate in some aspect of the ceremonies. According to the organizers, the rigidity of the Wenakuo is designed to promote a level of learning, discipline, and respect for others not possible when individuals are under the influence of popular gay culture. Although most people agreed with the regulations, by the end of the ten-day camp most people had grown weary of the regimen, and some would leave early out of fatigue and in some cases disdain. As Andy reminded me, "Wenakuo is not where you come to meet partners, have sex, or be gay. It is where you come if you are called to learn and walk the path that is intended for you."

At my first encounter with the concept of the gathering, the planning process of the first nationally advertised Oklahoma retreat revealed different views people had about the content of gatherings. For the most part the Oklahoma gathering represented a social occasion for Two-Spirits from around the country to come together, socialize, learn about other traditions, "snag" and develop relationships. Although the Oklahoma group had sponsored retreats in the past for Two-Spirit people within the state, this was the first time they invited people from all over North America. I started my project with the Oklahoma group about six months before the retreat, and soon after my arrival was incorporated into the planning and fundraising efforts. The group's primary concern was finding the money to cover the cost of the camp and food so the attendees' only financial responsibility would be getting to the camp. The agency that funded the men's group and the clinic would not allow funds designated for the group to be used for the retreat. Determined to find the money, we held garage sales, raffled a star quilt my mother made, took up collections at every meeting, solicited funds from gay-friendly churches, and generally scrounged for every penny. The group was able to raise the funds, plus some extra, to pay the costs of the gathering. In all, 40 people, mostly from the central and western United States, attended the retreat. Included in the activities were a "no-talent show" predominated by loungelike drag acts, talking circles, hikes, stomp dancing, hand games, and, on the final night, a powwow and giveaway.

In 2000 the Green Country Society invited gay Native men from all over North America through a significant mailing, e-mail, and public outreach effort. The 2000 Oklahoma gathering was significant for several reasons. First, the group had to raise 80 percent of the money for the gathering because the clinic refused to fund an event open to men outside Oklahoma. Planning and fundraising for the retreat brought the Two-Spirit group together into a cohesive cooperative social unit, and the Gathering became a point of pride for everyone involved. Second, the Gathering transformed the Eagleton group from a regional

Two-Spirit organization to one of national renown. That is, the 2000 Gathering was so successful that in 2001 they had to turn people away from advance registration.

The Green Country Society makes a concerted effort to create a welcoming atmosphere for people from multiple tribal backgrounds and levels of traditional participation by having events such as a drag show and a traditional powwow. The Oklahoma Gathering is also popular due to the level of hospitality. The GCS provides housing in cabins and brings in professional cooks for the meals. Participants are only responsible for their transportation to and from the gathering. The gathering itself has a fairly relaxed atmosphere with a few scheduled presentations on HIV/AIDS, self-image, relationships, and substance abuse. In recent years, Native celebrities have come to the gathering to give presentations on Saturday afternoons. Gathering participants are expected to help wash dishes and keep things clean around the camp area. Most of the gathering is spent socializing, making and learning crafts, hiking on the nearby trails, and participating in small ceremonial activities.

The gathering begins on Friday afternoon as GCS members hurriedly set up the registration table, put food away, and smudge off the ten or so cabins at the campsite. As cars pull into the gravel parking lot, friends are met with choruses of "Lululu!" and "Sister!" and hugs from the waiting group. Many of the people who attend the gathering have traveled from the Two-Spirit societies of Colorado, Minnesota, Texas, Kansas, and Washington, while other people, who heard about the gathering through the Internet, come from reservation areas in Montana and the Dakotas where they have little opportunity to be around other gay Native people. By dinnertime on Friday, most of the participants have arrived and the excitement of the gathering participants is overwhelming.

Two-Spirits Rising

Two-Spirit social relations are founded on the goal of self- and social acceptance, which many gay and lesbian Natives feel cannot be found in mainstream Indian society. As we will see throughout this book, self- and social acceptance are inextricably linked in the life of GLBT Indians.

The hostilities, both explicit and perceived, toward same-sex desire and gender difference among Native peoples greatly affects individual access to cultural practices, while the hostility toward individuals of color among the gay community affects access to social and sexual participation. Therefore, the desire of gay and lesbian Indians to participate in their culture and be accepted by individuals who share that culture is to a great extent responsible for the appearance of Two-Spirit identity.

In the following chapters I will explore the ways Two-Spirit identity is conceived of through the complexities of the social, political, and personal struggles of men who identify as both Indian and gay. Scholars have previously attempted to discredit (Epple 1998; Goulet 1996) or limit (Thomas and Jacobs 1999) definitions and use of the phrase Two-Spirit because it lacks tribal specificity and is felt to be only applicable to urban gay Indians. However, these disagreements appear to be largely academic and reveal very little of the "on the ground" ways that Native gay men use the term as a reflection of self and their social engagement. Since the mid-1990s when the term was becoming widely used among GLBT Indians and the late 1990s when academics began publishing on the term and concept, Two-Spirit has become a term that embodies multiple cultural themes (local, tribal, and mainstream Indian) and various gender conceptions (gay, lesbian, bisexual, and transgender). The term has gained status as a political moniker and, in the true test of a lasting concept, has been appropriated by non-Indians. GLBT Native scholars and scholars who study GLBT Natives may be engaged in discussions about the appropriateness of Two-Spirit as a term and its specificity as a descriptive idiom. Yet the men in this book are engaged in defining how the term Two-Spirit embodies their cultural, racial, sexual, and gender identity. They are further engaged in defining the social world of Two-Spirit through a creative engagement with their own sex and gender identities, as well as that of their tribes and the Native community at large.

CHAPTER THREE

Adapting to Homophobia
among Indians

All of the Two-Spirit men in this book have had to, at one time or another, keep their sexual orientation a secret or attempt to "pass" to avoid bringing attention to their difference. Two-Spirit men have dealt with this necessity in various ways, both within Indian and non-Indian social contexts, such as denying one's orientation or "butching it up" to feign hypermasculinity. This division is not much different than the experiences of non-Indian gays who live with a "secret" kept from families, employers, and friends. For the Two-Spirit man, however, the divided life is exacerbated by growing up knowing that the tribal identity emphasized by one's family and community does not include same-sex desire. As they grew up, the men I talked to were made distinctly aware that homosexuality was not an acceptable human characteristic and especially not an acceptable part of Indianness. In previous chapters we learned that the term Two-Spirit gave the men a way to resolve this division, but outside Two-Spirit social contexts this reconciliation is largely metaphorical. The men in this book feel that their tribal communities and Native society as a whole remain hostile to their sexual orientation and gender difference, so for reasons of self-preservation they must keep their racial identity separated from their sexual identity when among other Indians.

Homophobia among Native peoples has required Two-Spirit men to construct a division between Indian social worlds and their sexual orientation and gender identity. This division becomes reflected in the adaptations that most Two-Spirit men have learned to use when dealing with non-gay Indians. Men participate in Native social events such as powwows and go to ceremony, but do so within the expectations of "male" members of that community, not as Two-Sprit men. Hiding their identity during their participation is seen as not equivalent to participating as a Two-Spirit person. That is, men feel that they are being held to the standards associated with anatomical sex versus their sexual and gender identity. The desire to participate as a Two-Spirit person is complicated by the lack of specific cultural practices incorporating their difference. Accordingly, their frustration with not being incorp- orated is exacerbated by their knowledge that, historically, men who shared their differences were publicly inducted into Native societies, as well as given positions of prestige.

I purposefully do not focus on information derived from non-gay Indians. Because this book is about the ways Two-Spirit men experi- ence being Two-Spirit, I feel that it is appropriate to focus on the ways they see themselves in relation to non-gay Indians, their families, and larger Native social values as well as the ways that they actively attempt to adapt to a social environment they perceive as hostile to their identity.

Witnessing a Contradiction

Recent academic writing stresses the acceptance of gender diversity in historic and contemporary Indian communities. However, the major- ity of Two-Spirit men I encountered had multiple negative experiences with their fellow tribespeople and Native people in general surround- ing their identity as gay and Two-Spirit.[1] Some Two-Spirit men do ac- tively participate in their communities and are assumed to be gay by friends and family, but they are seldom open about their sexual orienta- tion out of fear of alienation. Two-Spirit men assume that openness about their orientation will assuredly negate any respect, status, and privileges afforded them within tribal society. Therefore, a significant problem arises when individuals desire to participate in their commu- nities while desiring to be open about their sexual orientation. Two- Spirit people's feelings of alienation are exacerbated by the assumption that non-gay Indians will judge them according to their sexuality and gender orientation, not their commitment to the preservation of Native ways of life.

Despite the academic reworking, interpretations of Native American gender diversity ignore the significant role that dominant conceptions of same-sex desire play in contemporary Two-Spirit identity. Almost every Two-Spirit man I met, talked to, interviewed, and spent time with emphasized that his/her identity was less about sexual orientation and more about being Native. At the same time, Two-Spirit men are very vocal about the ways homophobia affects their participation in tribal activities such as ceremonies and powwows. Scholarship on gender diversity is highly critical of conceiving Native gender diversity solely in terms of sexual orientation (Blackwood 1984; Jacobs et al. 1997; Lang 1998; Roscoe 1998; Thomas 1997; Thomas and Jacobs 1999; Williams 1987). I also agree that we should avoid characterizing Two-Spirit people based solely on their sexual orientation. However, we must also recognize that Two-Spirit sexual identity is the basis upon which they are alienated from social belonging and fear being denied access to social participation among Native peoples. When faced with the possibility of being denied access to tribal social circles, it is sexual orientation that becomes the determining factor for many Two-Spirit men. Although Two-Spirit people do not see their identity as comprised only of sexual orientation, they are aware that most Indian people do. Overcoming bias against their sexual orientation becomes a monumental barrier in gaining access to tribal social and ceremonial circles as well as to Native society at large. It is obvious that the recognized prejudice against gays and lesbians among many Indians acts to frustrate Two-Spirit men's desire to be active members in their respective Indian communities.

Two-Spirit men's experiences are influenced by dominant perceptions and actions of aversion toward their sexual desire. In order to understand the role of desire we need an examination of desire as something more than that felt by Two-Spirit men, but also as a conception through which relations of inequality are acted out. Inevitably, Two-Spirit men's relationships to the Indian social circles in which they seek to participate will be affected by a discernment of qualities other Indians seek to emphasize, "gayness" not being one of them. Accordingly, what we must understand is that the "problem of desire" also resides in the ways that Two-Spirit people perceive and experience non-gay Indian bias against their sexual desire. This bias is generated in the ideals that allow non-gay Indians to equate Two-Spirit people with their sexual desire rather than with their desire to be full members of their community. Non-gay Natives equating Two-Spirit people with their sexual orientation frustrates Two-Spirit desire for social belonging. Two-Spirit social life makes problematic the whole of desire. The whole of desire is not only sexual desire but also individual longing for self-acceptance, acceptance in their communities, and a socially affirmed identity that represents how they see themselves. Accordingly, dominant perceptions of sexual desire complicate the fulfillment of the men's desires, such as socially participating in one's tribe.

The social participations in question are found in the important roles within tribal society, such as head lady dancer, Stomp Dance leader, medicine person, and elder. These identities of prestige are subject to judgments of "appropriate" behavior. Even everyday roles such as jingle dancer, singer, and beader are permeated with performative stipulations. Two-Spirit people, in an attempt to meet the requirements of these identities, spend a significant amount of time making regalia, learning songs, and going to ceremony; that is, being Indian. Nevertheless, most feel that despite their best efforts they cannot perform these roles within tribal society due to intolerance for their sexual identity. That is, they perceive the hostility from non-gay Indians toward their sexual identity as overshadowing their achievements of cultural knowledge and practice. Most people are well aware that public recognition of their sexual orientation and gender identity would not allow access to particular positions in Indian society. Therefore, anxiety over homophobia and alienation causes many people to keep their orientation a secret. Staying in the closet for self-preservation becomes the only option for many Two-Spirit men who want to participate in social and religious communities. Most individuals who are open about their gender transgressions and sexuality are publicly and privately rebuked or simply ignored.

Two-Spirit men's attempts to relocate a place for themselves in Indian culture are exemplified by the ways in which they actively pursue participation in mainstream and tribal society, and by the ways they attempt to reconcile community perceptions of same-sex desire with a desire to participate socially. Most of the Two-Spirit men represented in this book sought participation in tribal and Indian social circles such as powwows and ceremonies. However, their participation turned on the fear of being a target of homophobic behavior or outward acts of hostility by non-gay Indians. Fear over the denial of ceremonial and social access overwhelmingly governs how Two-Spirit men behave in public, as well as with whom they associate at public gatherings. Their awareness of the ways non-gay Indians construct Native identity influences the ways in which they see themselves. By being gay, lesbian, or Two-Spirit, individuals run the risk of not being accepted by the people with whom they desire to socially interact. The Two-Spirit goal of representing themselves as faithfully embedded in tribal tradition emphasizes their sameness with mainstream Native peoples, while simultaneously they seek acceptance of their differences. Attempts at associating Two-Spirit with modern conceptions of "Indian" are frustrated amid dominant community regulations on available interpretations of Native male identity.

The contradiction exists not only in the ways the academic literature has romanticized contemporary Native gender diversity, but also in the lack of acceptance given them by their fellow tribespeople. Survivability is a focus of many tribal efforts to improve health, education, and traditional teachings. What puzzles Two-Spirit men is that their families and tribes create a hostile environment for people who are willing to sacrifice time and effort to increase the survivability of culture and young people. Ben bemoans, "They are talking out of both sides of their mouth. They say they want our people to survive and culture to live but don't allow us to be who we are. That doesn't make any sense. They are losing out on our contribution."

An "Indiscriminate" Change in Values

Two-Spirit men's recognition of sociohistorical influence on sexuality and gender ideology does not excuse Native people from their current points of view. Two-Spirit men are surrounded by tribal members who speak reverently of the traditions of the past and how realignment with the old ways would cure the ills of Indian people. At the same time they understand that the tradition of gender diversity is one that most Indians do not venerate or wish to revive. They also hear Indian people rebuke colonialism and the political-economic situation caused by European intervention in the same breath that these tribespeople apply

Western value judgments on their sexuality. For most of the men in this book, Native people's resistance to accepting Two-Spirit men represents an indiscriminant acceptance of non-Indian values. Two-Spirit men locate the beginnings of a change in attitudes toward difference in the Indian community with the wholesale acceptance of Christian values.

— Sean: *Christianity has had an enormous amount of influence on the Indian community. They [Indian society] have Christian beliefs that homosexuality is wrong and they don't feel that we have a place because of it. If they continue to look at us that way, then we cannot fulfill our traditional role.*

More important than sociohistorical changes in attitudes toward difference is the insistence that Indian acceptance of Euro-American values alienates Two-Spirit people from their traditional right to participate in tribal society as gender-different people.

— Glen: *We are limited in expanding our religious role to people outside of the Two-Spirit community because Europeans have influenced our people so much, they have gotten away from their own traditions. When the Two-Spirit people who are open come to them and say, "I can do this, I know these songs," and whatever else, the community closes them out. Because they have been influenced by the Christian churches to think that we are evil, and they say, "No, we can't have a Two-Spirit person up here doing that because we've gotten away from that tradition."*

— Ben: *When you had a society or tribe that supported the Two-Spirited they helped you to achieve your spiritual goals. Here we are being constantly knocked down for it. Two-Spirit has become a negative connotation in the Indian community. Back then [historically] it was a positive connotation. We were taught that whatever was different was not negative, it was seen as a gift. Today we are constantly having to get into people's faces and struggle.*

—Sean: *In the past, with our ancestors, Two-Spirit people actually had an important place in society where they would conduct ceremonies. They were accepted and had a part in everything. I feel that we don't have a role right now because we are not approved of anymore.*

— Glen: *Dominant society has such a hold on Indian people. And a lot of Indian people refuse to acknowledge these things [the existence of Two-Spirit people]. They want to pick and choose the traditions that sound good to white people and make them look good to white people. They say, "We can't tell them about the Two-Spirit tradition, because they are evil." They feel like they have to leave the Two-Spirit people out because of the influence of the church and white values. So it is going to be very hard for Two-Spirit people to find their way back.*

The condemnation of sex and gender differences rendered most Two-Spirit men socially invisible or the objects of misunderstanding. Attitudes expressed by Sean, Ben, and Glen are on the whole representative of the way that many Two-Spirit men felt about Indian adoption of cultural values. The transition from incorporation to condemnation amounts to what they see as a cultural betrayal. Most Two-Spirit men considered the adoption of Christianity by Native society as indiscriminate and thereby creating a dichotomy between traditional values and the ones that currently alienate them.

— Glen: *We didn't lose these traditional ways on purpose. They were forcibly taken from us. I heard this old man talking one time, and he said when the white people used to come, they would ask, "Who are your Two-Spirit people?" Then they would kill the Two-Spirit people, because their church said that they were evil. And then they came to the next village and they would say, "We don't have Two-Spirit people." They were saying that to protect their Two-Spirit people. They had to hide their Two-Spirit people. So because they hid them, they didn't get to participate in ceremonies. Also, white society has influenced Indian society to the point that they took these roles away from Two-Spirit people. The Two-Spirit people were tired of fighting so they just gave in.*

— Sean: *Stigmatism on homosexuality is at the heart of the decline in our roles. But also I consider myself a woman. I feel like a woman. I like to do womanly things like crafts. Somehow that is seen as bad also.*

Although most tribes by the early part of the 20th century no longer publicly incorporated gender-diverse traditions, Sheila grew up in one of the few reservation communities where elderly tribal members acknowledged Two-Spirit men well into the early 1980s. Unlike most Two-Spirit people, Sheila has been a witness to the decline in the traditional acceptance of Two-Spirit men.

— Sheila: *In the old days, when I was a kid, I would go visit the Two-Spirit people because they were always doing arts and crafts. They would tell me about different plants, ceremonies, and gossip. Nowadays there's a breakdown in traditional society. A lot of it has to do with the upbringing of kids. And traditionally winktes were liked by people because we were the babysitters of the tribe and we took care of the kids. People would leave their kids with Two-Spirit people, because they could trust us and we taught their kids about being Indian. People now don't instill this traditionalism in their kids.*

I can tell when a kid has been raised traditional. They respect me and don't give me a hard time. The traditional people are respectful at powwows. But I have had to leave powwows before because people weren't traditional. Nobody wants to stick with what traditions worked and what was there before.

Sheila's sister Wanda adds:

I think because of the decline of the Native culture, the language, the traditions with my parents and today's youth, they don't understand that several hundred years ago with most tribes in North America there were Two-Spirit people. And because they don't understand it they fear it.

Because the gender different were hidden or no longer accepted as a public identity, people did not have exposure to them. In effect, the change in contact with traditional roles through time isolated not only the Two-Spirit person but also the concept of the Two-Spirit person. In one example, Sheila detailed to me how some of her older uncles and cousins had to stay "in the closet" while living on the reservation. She told me that everyone knew that there were gay men, but "no one ever acknowledged it. It was something that people didn't talk about." When one of her uncles began losing weight and became chronically ill, no one spoke of the disease AIDS. When he died, family and friends referred to him as having "cancer." Sheila attributed intolerance, as the result of a loss of tradition, as the primary cause of the secret life that her uncle had to lead. She also blamed the lack of public roles for his getting HIV/AIDS. Since there was no place for him as a Two-Spirit person in tribal society, he had to turn to the gay community to "express that side of himself."

The decline in the practice of socially incorporating sex and gender difference is the result of changes in cultural practices making the role of the Two-Spirit incompatible to modified customs.[2] Modifications produced ceremonial and social roles where sex and gender difference were seen as not pertinent, necessary, or desirable. Glen gives us an example:

One of my Pueblo friends, her grandfather was a medicine man. When he was retiring because of age, he gave his duties and knowledge to a Two-Spirit man. She remembered her grandfather telling her that she must treat that Two-Spirit person with respect. But since then, so many of the old ones have died and the younger people have taken over, and they make fun of that Two-Spirit person. They don't respect him and have taken those roles away from him. I know it is the influence of school, churches, and TV.

Although Two-Spirit men share the general view that Indian people are victims of colonialism and pressures to acculturate, they are also critical of tribal leaders for not holding on to traditions of gender diversity as they did other cultural practices. In this way, Two-Spirit men see the respect once given gender diversity as a part of the historic traditional values that Indian people now venerate. In contrast, many non-gay Indians see same-sex relations and gender difference as something that did not exist historically and should not be recognized as associated with contemporary Native peoples. The ways in which Indians view sexual orientation, as well as the ways Two-Spirit men perceive other's perceptions of their sexual orientation, are explicitly tied to modern conceptions of popular "white" gay culture in America. Non-gay Indians have difficulty reconciling what they perceive as modern American gay identity and social roles in historic Native communities. This obvious disassociation between what is considered "white" and what is considered "traditionally Indian" creates a significant disagreement over the place of gender diversity in contemporary Indian society.

On the whole, mainstream and tribal Indian ideas emphasize same-sex relations as specifically not in line with traditional values. To quote one tribal chairman: "It is totally opposite to our traditional teaching and religion, which is based on a strong family life. I don't want those two (words 'gay native') put together. It's a disgrace to put them in the same category" (McLeod 1998:2). Sheila's sister Wanda comments: "I can't think of one traditional Native community where Two-Spirit people are still respected for the roles that they have, like a hundred years ago. Mostly this is because being gay in mainstream America is a taboo. Even now Indian people have a hard time hearing someone say that they are 'gay' or 'Two-Spirit.' They are afraid because their own people don't understand them."

Ben felt that most of the men's parents equated their son's identity with stereotypical images of gays and lesbians as promiscuous sexual deviants. Parents often failed to recognize their son's sexual orientation as something positive, and for the most part refused to see it in terms of historic gender diversity traditions. Ben summed it up: "Most people don't want to think of Indian men as queens or stereotypes about unhealthy gay people and most people do not want to recognize a historical place for Two-Spirit men based on their sexual orientation."

Most of my non-gay Indian acquaintances see same-sex relations as something specifically in opposition to traditional Indian values. One afternoon I questioned Rob, a non-Two-Spirit Puebloan man, with whom Ben and I often gourd danced, about his views on Two-Spirit men. His attitude was not one of extreme homophobia. However, his statement along the lines of "I don't care what they do, just so it's not in my backyard" indicates how some people perceive gay and lesbian Indians. That is, any recognition of gayness as a human quality is one that belongs not in the public sphere, but one that should reside out of civic view. In conversations that occasionally turned into heated discussions between myself and others, many people explicitly indicated that there was not a place for "that kind of behavior" in traditional Indian social life. When I inquired as to what "that kind of behavior" entails, most people drew on public displays of affection by two men, such as kissing or holding hands, and men dressing as women or acting feminine. In the event that public roles such as Stomp Dance leader or lodge pourer were mentioned, a lot of non-gay Indians saw that as merely an Indian man performing male tasks. Therefore, there was an explicit disassociation between the holistic way Two-Spirit men see themselves and the ways they were potentially seen by other Indians. When non-gay Indians heard the term or concept Two-Spirit, they almost always associated it with same-sex relations, or cross-dressing, which was framed as specifically inappropriate behavior for an Indian man. A public role for Two-Spirit men would inevitably involve recognition of them as different. A positive public association with Two-Spirit men would involve an unconditional recognition of their difference in Indian community values. Such a change seems daunting when confronted with what one Indian woman told me: "They can be gay, they just don't need to flaunt it." And when I told this to Sheila she replied, "So flaunting it to them just means living to me."

The winter 2000 edition of GCS's *Two-Spirit News* led with the article "Two Spirits Respected in Indian Tradition: Indians Have Tradition of Respect for Gays." On several occasions, tribal administrations returned the publication with notes about never sending it to them again. Ben frequently mentioned some of the overwhelmingly negative notes that were attached to returned newsletters where pejoratives such as "fag" and "homo" were often employed. I also heard of incidents where notes were left on tables in the clinic outreach booth with a similar intent. On one occasion Ben returned to the booth at a powwow on a Saturday morning to find an owl feather lying on the table. The association between owls and death is well known in Indian Country, and Ben took this to have a clearly hostile meaning.[3] Acts such as these were perceived by Ben and others as representations of Indian people losing touch with their traditional values – not only with Two-Spirit men being traditionally revered, but as Ben stated, "the lack of respect for the ways Indian people used to treat each other."

Come Out to Where?

A further complication was created around the issue of coming out. During my research, one of the Oklahoma members, Jeff, came out to his mother. Jeff had lived an openly gay lifestyle in college, and after graduation moved to a major metropolitan city in the south where he continued to be openly gay. However, he felt that he needed to be closer to his family, tribal community, and his cultural practices. He moved back to the rural area where he grew up not far from Eagleton and began working with an Indian youth organization. When I first met Jeff he had not yet come out to his mother. He was seriously committed to another Indian man who lived in a nearby city. They were maintaining a long-distance relationship but desired to live in the same place. It was at this point that Jeff felt it necessary to be open with his mother and aunt. Eventually, Carl and Jeff moved into Jeff's rural home together. I was surprised at the level of acceptance that Jeff's mom, Sally, and his aunt Louise gave his relationship. However, Jeff and Carl remained in the closet as "roommates" to the remainder of the family and to the people in the small rural community where they lived. During a GCS powwow gathering, Sally got up during their family's giveaway and gave a moving speech about Jeff and his coming out. She told of how she had no choice but to accept this: "Jeff is my son, and it is the way the Creator intended it." She went on to say that despite being saddened by the possibility of not having grandchildren, she was getting another son with Carl. The room was full of teary eyes and smiling faces, and Sean leaned over to me and said, "My mother would never get up and say something like that."

About six months after Sally's speech at the gathering I got to meet Calvin's parents. We were all traveling to a powwow in a nearby state and his parents' house was on the way. We were not staying overnight but merely stopping for a visit. Calvin has been out to his parents for about five years, and during that time they have grown to tolerate, as he puts it, his sexual orientation. Calvin considers his parents very religious (Christian) and generally intolerant of gays and Indians, despite being Native themselves. They knew that Calvin was bringing his Two-

Spirit friends over to visit that day. When we pulled up the gravel drive, his father was standing on the porch. All six of us piled out of the van and he came over to talk with Calvin. As Calvin introduced each of us, his father just stared with no motion at each of our extended hands, an obvious slight in Indian Country or anywhere else. We eventually moved inside and talked for about an hour in the living room. As we were leaving down the long driveway, his father yelled from the porch, "My granddaddy used to shoot homo Injuns." Ben replied, "I just may come back and shoot you."

Jeff and Calvin's experiences barely touch upon the ways various attitudes and consequences are manifest when one is open about one's sexuality to family and friends in the form of "coming out" or "being out." For Calvin the consequences were twofold. Despite being enrolled members of a Southeastern tribe, Calvin's parents considered themselves Indian only in terms of heritage and not social associations and religious practice. Not only were Calvin's parents bothered by his sexual orientation, but they were also hostile to his "Indianness." Calvin felt that his strong identification with being Indian only acted to exacerbate his parents', especially his father's, feelings toward his gayness. Conversely, Jeff's mother and aunt, who are fully incorporated into the social life of their tribal and ceremonial community, went to great lengths to encourage his recent expression of gender difference, albeit out of broader tribal and extended family view. They supported his learning female ceremonial roles, and on occasion held private family ceremonies where he could practice those roles. He told me, "It is really hard being Two-Spirit in a small Indian community. Without the support of my family and friends, I probably wouldn't be dancing and singing."

The experience of coming out for the men in this book varied depending on the individual. Most ideas of coming out included coming to terms with the difference that one's same-sex desire represented on a personal level, telling one's family and close friends that they were gay, or being "loud and proud." Most men gave vivid detail of their coming-out experience, which inevitably involved telling close friends and family that they were gay. On the whole, men in both groups had generally come out to their family when they were in their late teens or early twenties. In most cases family members were distraught about what they saw as their son's "choice."

Consistently, "being out" and "coming out" are significant situations of anxiety for Two-Spirit men. They recognize that being out complicates their desire to participate in the public and modestly small world of Indian society. Coming out has a significant emphasis in the popular gay community not only as a way to personal acceptance, but also as a political statement about the status of gay and lesbian people in Western society. In gay society, coming out is intended to emphasize and celebrate one's difference. By being out, an individual sets himself apart from the mainstream heterosexual ideology. On the other hand, the act and the concept of coming out as a gay person in the Indian community is for the most part unintelligible. That is, coming out in the gay community sense is explicitly associated with non-Indian society and values, leaving it as an unavailable means of social incorporation in Indian society. If the goal of coming out is to set oneself apart from the mainstream, then this would fail Two-Spirit goals. They do not desire to set themselves apart from their tribal identities and mainstream Indian society. Again, not setting oneself apart from their community is why Two-Spirit people attempt to separate themselves from images of mainstream gays. Ben stated that "many people just want to be themselves without fear. They don't want to come in like a big ol' queen and yell 'I'm here and queer.'"[4]

Mainstream Indian society has its own form of "coming out" for individuals wishing to be incorporated into cultural practices.[5] Frequently at powwows and ceremonies, an individual will be "brought into the circle" during their first performance as a dancer, singer, or ceremonial leader. Acts of public recognition are usually significant family affairs where notice is brought to an individual and their family for a brief moment. The family usually has a giveaway or a meal during the event to honor those who have influenced that individual's path into the circle. Public recognition in the Indian community acknowledges a woman's, man's, or child's solidarity with the Indian community, not their individual difference. That is, an individual becomes recognized as a productive member of that society. Males who are entering the powwow arena for the first time as dancers are wearing gender-specific regalia, are referred to as warriors, and are reminded by elders of their responsibility as men. Women who enter the powwow arena are similarly incorporated. Tribal communities often have "coming out" rites of passage for young women who begin their menses, publicly signaling their transition from child to women. Rites of passage, such as the *Kinaalda* among the Navajos, teach teenage girls all the customs and practices they need in order to be a member of adult tribal life.[6]

Two-Spirit men are quick to point out that Indian communities once had a mechanism for the incorporation and socialization of their differences from early childhood through puberty and into adulthood, thereby making the gay community form of coming out unnecessary. There is extensive historical evidence that Two-Spirit persons came by their public status as Two-Spirit through community and family observation as well as a series of rites of passage.[7] Therefore, the "causes" of an individual's proclivity toward gender-role change was not of primary interest in historic Native society.[8]

An individual's tendencies as a child toward certain gendered behaviors were observed by adults who eventually determined how that child's public identity would be formed. In the case of boys, this usually involved an interest in feminine-gendered activities and socially participating primarily with older females of the family and community. As Thomas points out for the Navajos, children having an interest in "work, tools, and activities associated with the gender opposite their sex often were encouraged to develop their interests" (1997:165). Inevitably, the demonstration of these interests, not only in the Navajo but in many tribes, would result in one eventually being publicly designated as a gender other than male or female. In other instances, boys who had dreams or visions where they were visited by spirits associated with a specific gender role were often recognized as belonging to alternative gender categories. In most cases there were specific rites of passage performed where an individual would be recognized as a mixed gender publicly and would from that point on begin the socialization process associated with that role (Lang 1998:218–239; Roscoe 1991:123–146; Williams 1987:21–24). Roscoe notes that, historically, Zuni men, women, and *lhamana* went through a series of ritual encounters with gender-specific symbols whereby individuals were initiated and publicly recognized into their gender status. In the case of lhamana, they were presented to society in a combination of women's and men's symbols to publicly recognize their third-gender status (1991:132–146). For the lhamana, public recognition of one's status was explicitly tied to a social position with specific signs and symbols intelligible to Zuni society.

In the Zuni example, the signs and symbols one is accessing must be associated with a particular social role intelligible to other Zunis. Coming out into tribal society, within the gay community interpretation, is rendered useless without public recognition of socially incorporated functions. That is, within the current ideology of most Indian societies, one would be seen as "coming out" as a gay person, not as a member of a community with a specific social position. Because the key element to acceptance is recognized social participation, the value placed on the coming-out process in the gay community to a large extent fails in the Indian context. As Jack told me, "There is nothing [roles] in our tribes for us to come out into."

Shame and Leaving Home

The greatest and most crucial commonality between Oklahoma and Colorado group members is not how they came out, but that they came out into the gay community, not in the Indian community. That is, most gay and lesbian Indians see the gay community as the only logical place for them to turn once they decide to be open with themselves, and to some extent their families, about their sexual orientation. Because Indian communities and families provide no mechanism for individuals to be socialized into their identity as gay, lesbian, or Two-Spirit, a significant number of Native gays and lesbians "come out" while they are living somewhere other than in their Indian communities. Men I interviewed felt that they had to move away from their families and tribal society in order to be "who they were" (placing an emphasis on their sexual identity). Generally, this involved moving to a major nearby metropolitan area and becoming absorbed in the gay lifestyle of that city. By moving, they felt that they did not have to draw attention to themselves or their families. Leaving home became a way to avoid negative attitudes and to be allowed more freedom to explore their sexual identity. Leaving home was a metaphor not only for moving away from their parents' home but also from their tribal, ceremonial, or church communities. Accordingly, upon returning home for visits or permanently, they often go back in the closet for fear of homophobia and being seen as shaming their families.[9]

Shame is often given as a reason for men to hide their sexuality. Among Two-Spirit men, and most of Indian society, shame is recognized as a way to restrict certain behaviors seen as doing potential social harm to one's family by drawing negative attention to oneself.[10] As everyone pointed out, how you behave is seen as a reflection of the way you are raised and the values of your family. If individuals behave in ways that the community disapproves of, then they run the risk of lowering their family's status in the community. Those who "shame out" their families may behave in ways judged inappropriate by the community, such as drinking at a ceremonial occasion or not fulfilling responsibilities valued by other tribal members, such as not taking care of one's family. Within the atmosphere of homophobia among tribal society, Two-Spirit men saw their sexual identity and gender difference as possible ways to shame their families. If a man were recognized as being homosexual, through an actual act or through rumor, he would bring negative attention to his family. The men saw this negative attention as having the potential to disrupt their family's status as well as their own, and to inevitably lead to their alienation. The men who came out to their parents were encouraged to keep their sexual orientation a secret and to "pass" for self- and familial preservation. For most men, the only way to reconcile their desire to be romantically involved with other men and remain in good standing with their family was to move away from home. Some men took advantage of natural moments of separation, such as looking for work after high school or going to college, as a way to remove themselves from the watchful eyes of family and community, while others became so fed up with hostility that they simply ran away.

Sheila had one of the most powerful and heart-breaking stories about leaving home. I knew a lot about Sheila before I actually met her. The GCS men had told me that she grew up in a well-known reservation family on the Northern Plains, that her father was politically and socially active in national Native politics, and that she was raised in a strictly traditional family. Because the men, and Sheila herself, emphasized her traditional upbringing, I assumed that she would be one of the few Two-Spirit people that had grown up as a mixed-gender person in a family that supported her role as such. However, I was surprised to hear that Sheila's family and community were mostly disapproving of her gender difference. From a very early age Sheila remembers preferring the company of her female relatives and learning "women's work." Her father, however, found his son's interest in female activities and feminine manner disturbing. As Sheila grieved, "He put me on a bronco horse when I was just ten and told me that I was going to toughen up; he wasn't going to have a sissy for boy. He often tried to beat it out of me."

By the time Sheila was in her early teens she was seeking refuge at her grandmother's home, wearing female clothes, and learning to bead and make dance regalia. Yet the pressure of being different in a tightly knit reservation community where her family had such a high profile led the teenage Sheila to run away to the closest city. It was living on the street in Minneapolis where Sheila found the freedom she was looking for among the other runaway teens. This freedom, however, came at a cost. Sheila began prostituting herself to other men almost immediately as a way to support herself. Sheila lived the street life for a few years before moving in with her mother, who had separated from her father and was living in Kansas. Living with her mother away from the reservation allowed Sheila to live as a woman out of the critical eye of her community, but also to, as she put it, "straighten out my life and get it together." Between that time and moving to Colorado, Sheila went to college and lived in various places throughout the western United States, making regalia and traveling the powwow circuit. Living off the reservation did not completely resolve Sheila's difficulties of being a man living as a woman. She cannot get legal documents such as a driver's license with her female name on it, and therefore cannot conduct her daily life as a woman, such as opening a bank account under her female name. The discontinuity between her legal name and gender and her appearance also make it difficult for her to find employment. Sheila pointed out that "all of these problems wouldn't happen if I lived on the reservation in the old days. They used to take care of their Two-Spirit people. And if I were welcome on the rez, I could make money by making regalia for dancers and I wouldn't need driver's licenses or social security cards. Everyone would know me and be ok with it." Because of the lack of acceptance but mostly because of the lack of incorporation of her difference on her reservation, "home" represents a place of hostility for Sheila. She said that she would return home if it were not so difficult for her to "pass" in a community that knows her family and knew her at one time as a boy. "They just make it really hard on me and others like me. They just stare, ya know," Sheila wept.

Sheila's overwhelming sense of being a woman complicates her life among her tribe and family in ways that other Two-Spirit men may not experience. The uniqueness of Sheila's story, however, does not alter the basic commonality she shares with other Two-Spirit men, in that their sexual orientation has required them to make certain life decisions that consequently separate them from the tribal and familial connections they cherish. In the most common story of leaving home, people "bide their time" by passing until they can leave their parents' house and support themselves. Several of the men, such as Ben, Sean, and Robert, all left home almost immediately after graduating from high school. Ben and Sean left home to attend regional universities, but were at least a four-hour drive from home, while Robert moved to a city to start an entry-level position in an advertising agency. All three men described these moves as necessary to get an education and begin supporting themselves, but they also described these moves as necessary for their peace of mind. As Robert explained further, "I came out to my mother before I left. She had no idea what I was talking about. She asked if I wanted to be a woman. I had to explain to her what it meant to be gay, that I was attracted to other men. It really caused a rift between us that still hasn't healed. I just had to get out of that little town and get some freedom."

Ben, as will be discussed in the next chapter, "went crazy" when he came out in college. He became absorbed in the college gay underground and the gay scene in a nearby city and consequently did not complete college. For Ben the move to college gave him an opportunity to react against his fundamentalist and homophobic upbringing. Leaving gave Ben an opportunity to, as he put it, "release all of that pent-up sexual energy I had been keeping down for my first eighteen years." Sean had a similar experience, albeit 20 years after Ben, when he began attending college. While Sean's post-AIDS-era promiscuity may not have been as reckless as Ben's, he too felt that the move gave him not only sexual freedom but also the freedom to be culturally gay. Sean reflected on that experience: "You know, I was totally in the closet everywhere but at school, and maybe I was only about half-out there. But I was definitely more willing to be as gay as I felt comfortable being. I was free to go to gay bars, marches, have coffee with other men, and it all not be a big deal. It was crazy once, my mom came to visit me at college and me and a friend ran around the apartment trying to de-gay the place taking down all the rainbow triangles and posters of half-dressed men. By the time we got done it looked like I had nothing but four blank walls."

Moving away gave the men opportunities to be gay in their sexual lives and to be involved in gay culture. Yet none of the men lacked regret for the necessity of their move. While Two-Spirit men see their communities as potentially hostile places, they also look to their tribes with a feeling of pride. They are proud of where they are from and who their relatives are, which makes their sense of alienation all the more troubling for them. They all grieved the cultural loss that came with leaving their communities and families. Most men returned for major tribal events, or to be with family during the holidays, but they lacked the experience of being a familiar adult member of their tribal society. They missed out on opportunities to be political and ceremonial leaders and to be available to their fellow tribespeople. Recently, Robert,

Sean, and Ben have all attempted to reincorporate themselves into their tribal communities as a way to reconcile lost chances at tribal involvement. However, their return has created a considerable amount of internal conflict for them. They have been used to living a much more open life concerning their sexuality, but find themselves having to revert to feelings of fear of homophobia and of having to hide their sexual orientation. Their greatest fear is that they will not be able to find their way back into tribal social life because someone will find out they are gay, or because they will not have the patience to continue to hide their sexuality. They have joined those men who stayed in their communities because they could not bear not being a part of tribal social life, but who remain in closeted isolation.

The Necessity of Passing

After the first couple of years going to tribal events and powwows with Two-Spirit men, I became adept at knowing when and where they were going to transform themselves into "straight-acting" Indians. When they would attend Indian social events, most of the men toned down the usually boisterous laughter that accompanied Two-Spirit social occasions. They also completely ceased any discussion of men, sex, or gay culture. Except for the very resistant, most Two-Spirit men participated in some form of "passing" behavior, whether it was changing their mannerisms, not using "gay talk," or changing their style of dress when around non-gay Indians. Passing is an important skill to master because it allows Two-Spirit men to participate in cultural and social practices without drawing potentially negative attention. By passing, Two-Spirit men are not only sheltering themselves from hostility but are also attempting to fulfill a personal need. That need is participation with their families, tribespeople, and friends. As many men have pointed out, if passing is the only way they will get to participate in tribal social events, then it is a justifiable necessity.[11] The need to pass can generate a substantial amount of distress for Two-Spirit men, as it requires one to continuously monitor his behavior. Only a handful of men I talked with would characterize themselves as "completely out" in every aspect of their lives. Being completely out is usually characterized by an individual affirming his sexual identity if asked by coworkers, friends, elders, and random people. Fears and assumptions about the reactions of people in the various social fields where Two-Spirit men participate determine whether or not they are open about their sexuality or gender status. Some individuals fear that their sexual orientation will be used by employers to fire them, or that it could make them subject to homophobic confrontations and violence. Yet access to Native ceremonial and social communities still represents the overriding concern for many Two-Spirit men. Denial of community access creates a prevalent predicament influencing the decision to pass as straight in Indian Country.

Over and over I heard men, particularly GCS members, express strong and worried reactions to the topic of being outed among one's tribal community and other Indians who had the potential to influence access to Native social networks. Being outed is where an individual unintentionally reveals his sexual orientation or is recognized as being gay by someone that he would prefer not know about it. Someone may be outed by being seen going into a gay bar or by someone "catching them in the act," such as holding hands or kissing another man. Also, someone may out themselves by saying something or behaving in a way that makes a connection to certain markers or behaviors associated with gay sexuality. Two-Spirit men are less worried about the latter forms of outing because they seldom encounter non-gay Indians in the places where they are socially gay. Rather, the men are most fearful of being outed through rumor. Therefore, Two-Spirit men are careful to not behave in ways that indicate gayness and are careful not to associate with individuals who are already known to be gay. They are most worried that speculation and gossip about their sexuality will determine the ways they are treated by their fellow tribespeople and potentially lead to their being denied opportunities to be actively involved in ceremonies and social events.

Robert and Todd were the most worried about the effects of being outed. The depth of this fear became all too clear one afternoon when I received an outraged phone call from Robert. Apparently Ben had sent out the *Green Country Two-Spirit Newsletter* to tribal headquarters across Indian Country, as well as to Indian social service organizations. The intent of the newsletter is to promote programs at the clinic with tribal governments and social service professionals. The newsletter contained numerous photographs from the GCS gathering where individuals, particularly Robert and Todd, were readily identifiable wearing their dance regalia. Many of the men in the photographs were not bothered by their outing in the newsletter. Todd and Robert, however, saw the newsletter as possibly generating rumors jeopardizing their attempts to continue their participation in tribal social and ceremonial circles. Both Todd and Robert were attempting to incorporate themselves into small tribal ceremonial communities and felt that if they were "found out" they would be denied access. In fact, Todd was rumored to have received a call from a tribal elder asking why he was in such a publication and associating with gay people.

The ways in which and reasons why Todd and Robert needed to avoid being outed was a common topic of conversation with both of them. Todd was worried about outing for multiple reasons. First, Todd was very active in an organization for Indian youth in his hometown. He feared that popular stereotypes about gay men as sexual predators would influence his continued participation in the program. Second, he was attempting to establish himself as a spiritual leader within his tribal society as well as to become a competition dancer on the pow-wow scene. He frequently reminded me and others that his "being outed" could threaten his standing in the community as well as his access to cultural participation. Todd also feared that if he were to be outed, his grandparents would find out about his sexual orientation, and as he put it, "That would just kill them dead right there."

Todd put a considerable amount of effort into keeping his sexuality a secret. He infrequently came to GCS meetings or activities but was often seen at powwows, where he would often ignore other Two-Spirit men who were also there. I noticed Todd's reluctance to sit with or socialize for long periods of time with Oklahoma members at public events. At one particular powwow Todd passed behind where we were sitting numerous times without saying hello. Some men took this as a slight, while others sympathized with Todd's difficult situation.

Some GCS members feel that their participation in their smaller, rural-based tribal and ceremonial communities makes them more conspicuous than they would be in the supposed urban anonymity of the Denver Society. Yet the Denver men often pointed out that they would be in the same situation as the GCS men if they were to return home. In the closely constructed tribal cooperatives, such as the ones to which Todd and Robert are seeking access, identity management is a crucial aspect of anyone's involvement. But for someone like Robert it becomes a practice that frames everyday life. Since my initial arrival in the Oklahoma society, Robert had talked about getting his regalia together to dance in his tribal war dance society. Being inducted into this society had a significant meaning for Robert. His grandparents had been involved in the tribal community, but his parents were not. His grandparents died when he was a young boy and he lost contact with his tribal community. As an adult, he was seeking reincorporation into tribal activities. Because none of his living male family members had been inducted in the war dance society and were not involved with the tribal community, he had to be sponsored by another family. Robert was adamant about his fear of being outed and not being allowed to participate in the community as a result. Robert's concerns about being outed led him to publicly and privately alienate many of the Two-Spirit men from the group. For example, when Ben announced that he was taking a van of people to the yearly war dance celebrations, Robert was very disconcerted and wary of being associated with GCS members. Previously, Robert had made the announcement at the GCS meeting that people from the group were not welcome at the camp of the family that was sponsoring him. However, an invitation from Robert was not necessary, since many men had invitations from other participating families. Therefore, many GCS members and myself went to the dances despite Robert's warning. Robert's anxiety over the mere presence of Two-Spirit men who he might be associated with was visible at the dances.

Robert expressed to me on several occasions that he felt conflicted about denying his Two-Spiritedness, but he reasoned that once he was inducted, being outed would be less of a threat. So, until he was accepted into the community, he had to be "extremely careful about being around other gay people."

Many Two-Spirit men adjust their associations and behavior according to community size, level of participation, and the degree of potential anonymity. More importantly, Two-Spirit men adjust their associations and behavior in reaction to perceived consequences, namely denial of access, within the Indian community.

Surveilled Masculinities

Fears about publicly and accidentally outing oneself leads Two-Spirit men to closely monitor their behavior as well as that of others. Two-Spirit men generally assume that their behavior will be judged according to masculinized standards. They take for granted that any behavior seen as transgressing community expectations will be met with hostility. Indian community conceptions about masculinity are assumed to be fixed, historically determined characteristics firmly grounded in popular and tribal notions of the "warrior." Emphasizing the image of the warrior as the quintessential Indian male relies on the decline of the actual social role of the warrior and on the romanticization of the warrior tradition, fixing it in time and space.[12] Native masculinity is assumed to have a certain set of historical claims and interpretations that specify what it means to be an Indian male. Accordingly, Two-Spirits, when reflecting on themselves, see these interpretations as more about what a contemporary Indian male is not than what he represents. They know, for instance, that the community associates feminine behavior and dress for men as explicitly not Indian. Two-Spirit men assume that they will be judged according to these masculinized community standards. The naturalization of racial difference into an essentialized category of male-bodied persons brings about an ideological framework against which Two-Spirits compare themselves. Two-Spirit men, in recognizing the homogeneity in community expectations of men, perceive no space for alterations in the performance of male Indian identity.

Most of the men I talked with saw behaving in flamboyantly effeminate ways, discussing explicitly gay topics, or using "gay talk" at Indian
public events as having the potential to be met with disapproval. The
distinction between behavior that the Indian community expects from
male-bodied persons and what many Two-Spirits see as part of their
gay identity leads to further alienation for certain individuals who do
not adhere to perceived Indian community standards. More than anything, perceptions of community surveillance of individual and group
behavior shape the ways in which Two-Spirit men behave in Indian
contexts such as powwows and ceremonies. This surveillance further
shapes the ways in which individuals perceive community expectations
of the performance of Indian identities. Many men readily invoke the
gay-community characterization of "butch" or "nellie" to describe individual and collective behavioral expectations. That is, individuals who
are seen as expressing typically masculine characteristics are known as
butch, and those expressing highly feminine characteristics are known
as nellie. The gradations from butch to nellie are determined by an
individual's clothing, mannerisms, tone of voice, and overall behavior.
The men I knew and talked to felt that most Indians had unwavering
expectations of men's behavior as butch, as well as a general condemnation for public displays of "nelliness."

Everyone was certain that overtly gay and alternatively gendered behavior, such as physical contact between two men, was explicitly out of
the question in Indian public space. Accordingly, examinations of individual behaviors usually did not focus on larger displays of gayness, but
instead were reduced to minute instances of individual mannerisms.
Occasions of transgressing community expectations were seen as having the potential to be perceived as disrespectful, or as drawing negative
attention to oneself or other community members. Being seen as acting
excessively flamboyant or "gay" or any transgression of masculinized
expectations would result in negative social attention. Negative attention drawn toward one person is then perceived as drawing negative
social attention to other Two-Spirit men. Negative attention toward
Two-Spirit men might also have the effect of outing someone who is in

the closet or wishes to remain anonymous. Therefore, Two-Spirit men critique and attempt to manage each other's public behavior in much the same way that a person who goes to a powwow drunk will be called down for it by an elder or the arena director.

Before going on a trip to a powwow or ceremonial event as a group, Ben reminds the men to "be respectful" because "not everyone is out." Being respectful means not drawing attention to oneself by being overly flamboyant and using gay talk. A distinct association is made between being seen or associated with stereotypical (white) gayness in an Indian context and potentially doing social harm to oneself or others. Many men associate "acting gay" with a kind of "disrespectful behavior" that will create a negative image of Two-Spirit men in the minds of non-gay Indians. Just as they do not want to breach social conduct rules themselves, no one wants to be associated with an individual who might violate them with behavior considered unacceptable in the Native community. Many men refer to behaving in socially inappropriate ways as "shaming out" themselves and their relations, including friends and family. Robert frequently complained about public attention being given to the more effeminate or flamboyant members of the group in Indian social contexts. When attending a powwow with the group, he would often go separately and spend the powwow walking around talking to people instead of sitting around the arena in folding chairs with the other Two-Spirit men. On numerous occasions he referred to being embarrassed by the flamboyant dress or mannerisms of certain group members and did not want to be associated with them publicly. Glen comments:

Traditionally among Two-Spirit people, there were the butch and nellies. There were very effeminate people, they were very flaming as you could say. But the people very much respected them because they know that was how the Creator wanted them to be.

When I first came out I was very condemning of effeminate people because I thought it perpetuated stereotypes. Now I have realized that everyone has their place in this world. Wherever you are you have to be real.

Some men saw any prohibition on their behavior in Indian contexts as running counter to their rights as a Two-Spirit person participating in community events. More importantly, some people would rather put the burden of intelligibility on the Indian community.

— Sean: *If they don't like it ["my behavior"] then leave me be. At pow-wows I try to behave as well as I can, even though sometimes when I get around the girls [Two-Spirit men] we start to cackling. I still try to be a little, well, I hate to say butching it up, but I try to behave. I put on my church attitude. If Indians are prejudiced toward me because of my behavior, then they are the ones throwing the circle out of balance, not me.*[13]

Overtly subjecting oneself to the judgments of Indian society was not a common practice for many people who attended public events. In fact, most were very careful about their impression management. Behaving in perceptibly nellie ways relied on a set of discourses intelligible to other Two-Spirit men, but remained unintelligible according to dominant public Indian behavior expected of men. Therefore, the lack of "camp recognition" or intelligibility of Two-Spirit community behaviors represents a significant difference when performed in mainstream Indian contexts.[14] For many, the risk of being unintelligible by the Indian community is far too great to risk "shame."

Consequences of Being Openly Two-Spirit

Conflicts within certain individuals about being openly gay in their tribal community and local Native society were often represented in conflicts over what "being out" represented for Two-Spirit men as a whole and individually. Generally, there are two opinions on being openly gay. Some see being openly gay in their communities as a positive move toward self-acceptance and a positive step for social and political progress for gay and lesbian rights. On the other hand, some individuals view being openly gay as potentially harmful to their social standing, family relations, employment opportunities, and safety. Glen commented, "I understand people being in the closet, although it doesn't help us. I have been fired from jobs and lost friends because I'm

openly gay. We still have to be who we are, though." Despite the consequences, several Two-Spirit men made a point of being open about
their sexuality and gender difference among other Native peoples.
These men challenge dominant Indian community control over the socially sanctioned content of Indian identity. Inevitably, they find themselves in a constant struggle for community access and recognition.

Indian communities use titles such as powwow princess, head man
dancer, or championship drummer and rewards such as powwow prize
money or honorings as a way to recognize an individual as an important member of the society. Access to such recognition and social participation is regulated within a dominant ideological framework that
seeks to legitimate a few Indian identities, for example, male powwow
singer and female Southern Cloth dancer.[15] For Two-Spirit men, the
forms of recognition and access to social participations are clearly embedded in heterosexual ideology. Identities such as female powwow
singer or transgendered traditional buckskin dancer (or simply gay Indian man) do not meet the ideological expectations among tribal communities or mainstream Native social circles. Therefore, Two-Spirit attempts to make their sexual orientation and gender difference a part of
their public Indian identity are usually met with confusion and hostility. Despite individuals meeting the symbolic requirements of female
jingle-dress dancing to the last detail, by being an anatomical male they
create a form of performance not intelligible in dominant Indian ideology. By being openly gay or transgendered, they run the risk of being
unintelligible to other Indians.

Again, simply by being a transgender Indian man, Sheila challenges
the gendered assumptions of most Indians, making herself subject to
the judgments of other Indian people. Shortly after Sheila moved from
Colorado to Jeff and Carl's house outside Eagleton, she began to jingle
dance in local powwows. By this time I had started going with Ben to
every powwow possible to gourd dance. We would often meet up with
Sheila, Carl, Jeff, and his family at powwows, and on occasion, all camp
together at an outdoor powwow. Ben and I met up with Sheila, Carl,
and Jeff and some other Two-Spirit men at a benefit powwow at a local
high school in Eagleton. Surprisingly, at least a hundred Indian people

were there in regalia to dance, which is rare for a small local indoor powwow with no prize money in the middle of winter. However, it was early December and people were starved for some sort of community participation. At this powwow I saw Sheila experience the greatest public slight I had ever witnessed in Indian Country. Sheila was an accomplished jingle, fancy shawl, and buckskin dancer. Not only is her regalia impeccable, but she put a significant amount of effort into perfecting and innovating dance steps. I was literally astonished by the degree to which she excelled over her competitors. At this particular powwow, Sheila had made a new jingle dress and was feeling particularly good about her recent performances. A few dances after the jingle competition, the emcee was going to announce the winners. However, there was a tie between Sheila and a well-known jingle dancer, Lana. The arena director ordered a dance-off between the two, and before the dance started, Lana went to the arena director and stated, loud enough for most of the gymnasium to hear, "But that's a man." The arena director acknowledged Lana's statement but seemed reluctant to make a scene, and the dance-off went on. Later, when the winners were announced, Lana came in first and Sheila came in third. Clearly, before Sheila was publicly recognized as a man she was competing for first place. We all stood in agitated amazement as Sheila walked out to receive her prize money and Lana gloated with a huge smile.

Sheila's perfection of jingle-dance regalia and performance became irrelevant once she was recognized as being anatomically male by the dance judges. Until the point of public recognition, people may have suspected she was male but might have been uncertain and unwilling to question it. However, once Lana made Sheila's transgression part of the public discourse, Sheila's performance became subject to the accepted signs and symbols associated with jingle dance, of which being a man is not one. Sheila continued to attend and dance in powwows during her year-and-a-half stay in Oklahoma, and she continued to butt heads with Lana, who seemed to be at every powwow we went to. Lana made an effort to stir up rumor and incited a rivalry that lasted for Sheila's entire stay in Oklahoma. In a moment of irony Lana won a jingle dress that Sheila had made and donated to a powwow raffle. We never did see Lana wear the dress to a powwow.

The day after the initial incident with Lana, Sheila went with Jeff and Carl to another local powwow so that she and Jeff (who competes in Fancy Dance) could dance. To no one's surprise, Lana was there in the gold jingle dress and we all expected there would be trouble. Throughout the evening Lana kept gazing at us while whispering to the other people sitting around her. Later during the powwow, as Sheila was lining up with the other dancers for the jingle competition, Lana came up and told her, "You don't belong here because the judges know you're a man." As Lana was beginning to create a scene, an older Cheyenne jingle dancer stood next to Sheila, scolding Lana: "Stop being a bitch and get your ass back in line." We were all pretty astonished by the public confrontation, but also by the amount of support shown by the dancer whom no one knew. Later that evening the Cheyenne jingle dancer came up to Sheila, introduced herself, and told us that "Lana doesn't know the old ways." During her dance career, Sheila has been disqualified from so many powwows it is "too many to count," and the support shown her by the Cheyenne woman is rare.

Two-Spirit men also encounter difficulties in attempting to gain access to "support staff" necessary to hold an Indian event. When the GCS decided to hire a drum to perform at the gathering powwow, I observed group members receive another saddening reminder of the prejudices against sexuality and gender difference in the Indian community. Having a "real" drum group for the powwow at the retreat was very important to the men in the Oklahoma group. The year before, many of the men who dressed in their regalia were also the only ones who knew how to powwow drum, so not everyone got to dance. Having professional drummers was also important because the group invited many gay-friendly non-Two-Spirit friends and family, bringing the number of participants close to 70. A "good drum" was a way to allow everyone to participate but it also lent a level of legitimacy to the Two-Spirit powwow.

Unless they are nationally known, drum groups are seldom offered more than $200 to be the center drum at a small regional powwow. Despite offering $400 for a two-hour set of songs to numerous drum groups, no one would commit to performing at the GCS gathering powwow. Ben contacted several singers he knew personally and relatives of drums that he knew. He was open with the head singers about the need to be respectful of the fact that they would be playing for gays and lesbians and that some would be cross-dressing in their regalia. Ben secured one drum through a friend, but three weeks before the gathering, the head singer canceled. He told Ben that his wife was accusing him of being gay because he was going to sing at a gay powwow. The head singer was also having trouble finding other people to "sit at the drum." Finally, Ben was able to get a random acquaintance to find a pickup drum and sing at the powwow.

The drum arrived late, which led everyone to joke that the late drum made the Two-Spirit powwow the "real thing." However, once everyone noticed the invited singers' attempts to hide their snickers, the good feelings about the drum dissipated. The head singer told Ben that they could only stay for an hour, as opposed to the four hours previously agreed upon. Also, the head singer demanded that a blanket dance be held in their honor. At most powwows a song honoring individual drums or singers is usually performed. A blanket is placed by the drum and participants throw money on it as they pass. Blanket dances are a sign of respect, but are also intended to help the volunteer drummers pay for the gas they used to get to the powwow. Ben was upset by their request for a blanket dance, because they were already splitting $450 four ways. However, Ben also felt that the drum was exploiting them because they were relying on them to provide music for the dances. More importantly, Ben felt that the drummers assumed they could exploit the GCS because they were Two-Spirit. Ben refused the blanket dance, and the drum group commented that he and the people running the powwow "were not Indian enough to know the right way." The drum group refused to continue to perform unless there was a blanket dance for them. Skip attempted to mediate on behalf of the drum group, telling Ben that it was proper for them to have a blanket dance.

Eventually Ben and Mick agreed, and a blanket dance was held, which only produced $11 for the drum group.

I was told by several people that the drum group would not have behaved in a "disrespectful manner" if the powwow were other than Two-Spirit. All people present, Two-Spirit or not, took the drum group's attitude personally and characterized their behavior as disrespectful. Even more egregious was Skip's siding with the drum group and drawing into question the cultural authenticity of the event. What seemed most devastating at the time was that the drum group's behavior acted to obscure Two-Spirit attempts at accessing the symbolic content of the Indian community. Having a "real" drum group perform was part of the Oklahoma group's attempt at conducting the Two-Spirit powwow according to Indian community standards. Inevitably, the drum group's behavior not only reminded Two-Spirit people of the lack of acceptance in mainstream Indian society but also denied them access to the same kinds of respect and participation expected in other Native communities. It also served to reinforce the need for Two-Spirit men to continue growing and investing in their own community and in the creative integration of their sexuality, their gender identity, and their Native cultural identity.

CHAPTER FOUR

The Aesthetics of an Identity

What Two-Spirit means, being of both male and female spirits, is almost never debated. But how to *be* Two-Spirit is something that elicits emotion, opinion, and at times outrage. I have seen the men in this book struggle with the various ways Two-Spirit is both a way to think of oneself and a set of ideals that one must meet. Ideals are complicated by the various cultural influences that have come to shape not only Two-Spirit men's lives but American Indians in general. For Two-Spirit men the struggle is to find a balance between the influences of popular gay culture and Indian culture. Having recognized that the gay community does not represent the Native aspect of their lives, Two-Spirit men are weary of "giving too much to the gay community." Also, realizing that their participation in most tribal communities would require keeping their sexual identity a secret, Two-Spirit men are reluctant to fully incorporate themselves into Native communities. Two-Spirit men must, as Ben put it, "keep one foot in the gay world" where their sexuality is accepted, and "one foot in the Indian world" where their cultural heritage lies. As Two-Spirit men now attempt to negotiate the two seemingly different aspects of their identities, as a community they encounter conflicting ideas concerning acceptance and belonging. In the search to discern the qualities that make Two-Spirit people distinct, gay indigenous men become subject to judgments about where they fit into the complicated social hierarchies of Indian and gay societies. Jack reflects on the dilemma of Two-Spirit identity and community:

Sooner or later we must figure out those qualities that define a Two-Spirited person in contemporary society. This self-definition is important for us and the future generations. It has to come from a cultural framework. By that I mean an Indian perspective whether it be from a mixed blood or full blood, who is urban or rural, and whose community of reference is a federal, tribal, and/or state land base. I believe it is not just content that matters, but context.

The struggle to define the cultural framework that Jack is speaking of

89

becomes a central dilemma in the lives of Two-Spirit men. The desire to be Native amid the homophobia of their tribal communities and the desire to be gay among a predominantly non-Indian gay community coalesce into an internal struggle for Two-Spirit men's social, political, and emotional allegiances. This struggle gets played out in the ways the men conceptualize what it means to carry the name Two-Spirit, but also what it means to *be* Two-Spirit.

Two-Spirits and Gay Indians

Sheila had temporarily moved from Denver to Jeff and Carl's house in rural Oklahoma. She came to Oklahoma with the intent of "getting herself together" and to start an Indian craft business with the couple. It had been six months since Sheila had moved to rural isolation, and she was longing for the gay scene she left Denver to escape. One winter evening, Sheila, Jeff, and Carl called me at work and wanted to come stay with me in Eagleton and "go out to the bars." We hit the usual gay hot spots around Eagleton. Later in the evening we ran into a group of five or so Indians at a western-theme gay bar. Jeff, Carl, and Sheila already knew some of them from powwows and the gay scene around Oklahoma. We ended up talking to them most of the night about things gay and things Indian, such as who you know, what style you dance, and for the Navajos, whether they were related. When the bar started to close down, Sheila took the liberty of inviting them all back to my house for a "49," which refers to the singing of social songs around a drum, usually with alcohol present. Forty-nine songs are either in English or have a combination of English and Native words and are about courtship, partying, or addressing contemporary Indian social issues through humor. Often after powwows, teenagers and single young adults will gather in a remote area away from the view of the older members of the community to sing, drink, and court each other.

Using the coffee table as a drum, we started pounding out songs and sang until the early morning.[1] One of the Navajo men was elated with our singing, but when someone handed him a drumstick he dropped it as if it were on fire, looking uncomfortable with us wanting him to participate. His naïve excitement over our singing amused everyone, but as I was to find out, it signaled something larger to the other people present. Later that morning at breakfast I asked Sheila what she thought about the Two-Spirit people that had come over, and she replied matter-of-factly, "They're not Two-Spirit, just a bunch of gay Indians." She went on to tell me that if they were Two-Spirit they would not spend most of their time "being gay" at the bars, and they would participate in the Two-Spirit community, as well as their tribal communities.

My evening with Sheila, Carl, and Jeff revealed two dilemmas. The first was the distinction individuals made between those persons who identified themselves as Two-Spirit and those who were perceived to be non-Two-Spirit, or rather, a "gay Indian." Accordingly, the relationship between gay Indian and Two-Spirit significantly mirrored distinctions frequently made between Indian and white/non-Indian. That is, the term and conception of Two-Spirit is reserved for individuals who chose to articulate their identity as gay not solely in the white-defined world of the gay bars and social scene, but within indigenous conceptions and social roles. Emphasizing Two-Spiritedness thus gives the mainstream gay community a secondary position in their lives.[2] The second dilemma was the conflict that many gay Indian men felt about participating in traditional Native practices with their tribes and families. This conflict precipitated mixed feelings about participating in anything Indian, including Two-Spirit society.

Early that morning at my house, under the declining beer buzz, our conversation became serious and turned toward an issue that always seems to be on gay Indian men's minds: acceptance. As the Navajo man, Carlos, began to cry uncontrollably as he told us the story of how his grandparents acknowledged that he was *nadleeh* when he was very young and tried to raise him with knowledge of his difference. Carlos's parents, however, were not involved in traditional Navajo culture but were fundamentalist Christians. Carlos bitterly recounted the ways his parents discouraged his participation in Navajo traditional culture and bombarded him with images of "hellfire for homosexuals." Carlos was angry because, as he said, he "knew there were once ways that my people would accept me and had for centuries." Through teary eyes he described the regret he had about not learning Navajo ceremonial ways from his grandparents. Carlos talked about going back to the reservation to learn Navajo practices, but he was not sure if anyone would accept him and wondered who would teach him. Like many Two-Spirit men who were raised with conflicting ideas about their sexuality and traditional practices, Carlos saw dealing with the Indian community as particularly threatening. As Carlos opened another beer and turned up the music, I sensed that he had talked himself out of his earlier excitement about Indians. It seemed that for Carlos, all things Indian represented a form of threat, while the gay community represented an easy tolerance. Sheila took a hard line, saying that she saw his attitude as a reflection of only identifying with his sexuality and not his culture. For Sheila, Jeff, and Carl, this was a dilemma that tugged at one's social, political, and personal allegiances, which also complicated what individuals thought about their own identity and the groups of people who had the potential to accept them.

Despite being aware of the experiences that shaped Carlos's attitudes about being gay and Indian, many Two-Spirit men had limited sympathy for what they saw as choosing the gay community over Indian ones. It is common for gay and lesbian Indian people to equate Two-Spirit with a code word or marker for being gay and indigenous; however, many of them had distinct associations between individual behavior and beliefs and being Two-Spirit. In most cases the division between Two-Spirit and gay Indian rested on the ideal ways in which people were perceived as conducting themselves socially and personally. Individuals seen to be making a contribution to an Indian community, Two-Spirit or not, through participation in Native culture and a clear allegiance to Indian people are more likely to be considered by their peers as fulfilling Two-Spirit ideals.

— Sean: *In my opinion you have to be in touch on a spiritual type of journey to find out who you are to be Two-Spirit. I've been out to the clubs before and seen people who I assumed were Native American that were gay. They're gay, but you never see them at powwows and gatherings like that. I don't really feel like they are [Two-Spirit], 'cause they are just relating as being gay. They don't acknowledge their Native Americanness.*

— Jack: *I agree that there are differing levels of involvement in community and that individuals have differing perceptions of whether they consider themselves "gay" or "two-spirited."*

— Ben: *The term Two-Spirit, to me, should be more of a sacred thing. If you're gonna carry that term Two-Spirited, you should be walking the talk and living it.*

Individuals who perform the required acts to be considered ideally Two-Spirit create a difference between those who are "culturally" and "spiritually" Two-Spirit, and those who fail to meet those requirements. Two-Spirit men emphasize their social and spiritual practices as something separating them from a strictly sexual interpretation of their identity.[3] However, the distinction between gay and Two-Spirit is considerably more complex than has been previously recognized. The men frame being Two-Spirit in terms of sexual identity as it articulates with the symbolic and behavioral requirements of being Indian. Access to the sign Two-Spirit becomes about more than sexual orientation to include a specific set of qualities recognized not only as Indian but also Two-Spirit.

— Andy: *For me, a Two-Spirit person is of Native blood, of Native culture, practices Native customs, and in some way contributes to the well-being of a Native community. Now, many people out there that are "Indian" and registered with one concentration camp [reservation] or another will call themselves Two-Spirit but have nothing to do with the Indian community. In fact, they are very "gay" or "lesbian" but culturally not very "Indian."*

Therefore, despite an individual having a Certificate of Degree of Indian Blood (CDIB), stereotypically Indian looks, or a well-known family, the failure to meet performative requirements could result in not receiving the designation of Two-Spirit by other Two-Spirit people. While the two components of being Indian and gay are required to be considered Two-Spirit, being an indigenous gay who is not culturally involved does not necessarily qualify one as Two-Spirit.

— Glen: *Two-Spirit is different than being gay. Two-Spirit is the traditional role that gay people held. All Two-Spirit people are gay, but all gay Indian people are not Two-Spirit, ya know? I think of the traditional role that Two-Spirit people played in our traditions and our old ways – the prayers, the storytelling, arts and crafts, the raising of the orphans, care for the older people. I see a lot of Indian people out at the bars and they say, "Oh, I'm Two-Spirit," and I just look at them and say, "Are you sure you're Two-Spirit or just a big ol' queen?"*

Often I was told of people who had stopped coming to the GCS bimonthly meetings, or had stopped coming to Denver ceremonial events, but were seen "out at the bars." Inevitably the information about the person is framed in terms of choosing to be "gay" over Two-Spirit, or "trying to be white/gay" over being Indian. Being involved solely in gay social circles meant turning away from one's Native heritage.

Two-Spirit men saw Indians who preferred the gay community as allying with the oppressive aspects of non-Indian society. By participating solely in "white" gay society, Indians were compromising themselves politically, culturally, socially, and personally. Gays and lesbians of color seeing the gay community as a white, oppressive institution creates a conflict of allegiances in terms of social participation.[4] Although many Two-Spirit people would rather not go to gay bars or involve themselves with the gay community, one's desire to be socially gay in order to find sex and partners can be an inherent conflict with one's desire to be socially, spiritually, and culturally Indian. Inevitably, the negative associations that the gay community invokes for Indians, such as racism and unhealthy living, is a factor in how individuals are perceived by other Indians, on which acceptance or alienation at times depends. People who are perceived as spending too much time in the gay social world can be declared as losing or lacking the special ability that Two-Spirit people presumably possess, such as clairvoyance or special relationships with the Creator. Accordingly, those who are perceived as giving too much to the white/gay community are seen as moving farther away from what it means to be Two-Spirit and Indian, and farther away from fulfilling their traditional roles in Indian society.

Two-Spirit and Traditional Responsibility

Distinctions about who is a Two-Spirit person and who is a "gay Indian" clearly draw upon the recognition of a contemporary connection with the historic roles of Two-Spirit ancestors and participation in traditional Native culture. Most gay Indians would quickly draw on historic tolerance and respect as a means to legitimize their sexual orientation. Conversely, Ben said, "Just because they accepted gays that doesn't mean that they're going to be like, 'Hey, queens, we love you now.' We have to be in the community." In this way, people saw individuals as significantly less Two-Spirit when they did not make an attempt to connect with Indian culture through developing skills as a medicine person, crafter, or performer, and when they did not make connections with an Indian community (of which Two-Spirit community is included).

— Lance: *Gay and two-spirited are, of course, not the same thing, since being two-spirited is a far broader concept than simply attraction to members of the same sex. The concept implies a way of life and a knowledge and acceptance of the responsibilities that that entails.*

The acceptance of Native ways of life is important in distinguishing oneself from gay society. Improving the quality of a person as an Indian entails choosing to emphasize one's ethnic identity over gayness through cultural practice and responsibility to a community. As Jeff told me, "It isn't enough to walk around and say 'Hey, I'm an Indian.'"

Two-Spirit people make an explicit connection between a commitment to Indian society and social and personal acceptance. Therefore, acceptance could only be gained through one's realization of responsibility through Indian and Two-Spirit community participation. Fulfilling one's traditional role encompasses not only being a member of a contemporary community, but accessing the known history of roles once performed by the Two-Spirit ancestors. Fulfilling traditional roles becomes translated to perfecting ceremonial knowledge, "women's work," and a commitment to participation in a community. Two-Spirit people have different ideas about what qualifies as fulfilling their traditional roles. For many people it means simply participating in Indian society on a social level. Going to powwows (and not dancing), being seen, and socializing are ways in which Two-Spirit people can participate in Indian society and not commit themselves to potentially time-consuming pursuits. Also, by participating minimally, individuals do not have to put themselves out there in forms of public performance. Many times individuals expressed anxiety over taking a role in public Indian events. In one example, we had been pushing Mick for over a year to gourd dance with us. Despite our offering to make his regalia, he refused to participate. He finally admitted that he wanted to wait until he got his "Indian card." The fear of rebuke over not looking verifiably Indian, combined with being gay, made him question being accepted in public performance and gave him much anxiety. Many members of both the Oklahoma and Colorado societies shared these fears. At times Two-Spirit people framed these fears as preventing individuals from fulfilling their traditional roles.

More active individuals, however, saw fulfilling traditional roles as specifically requiring the acquisition of knowledge and the transmission of that knowledge through active participation in Indian communities, Two-Spirit, tribal, and general. Active participation inevitably involved confronting many of their fears not only about homophobia but about what the Two-Spirit community saw as the Indian community's requirements of tradition.

— Ben: *Once you have established yourself in tradition then you can be given the opportunities to be a leader, be a spiritual guide or a namer. But you can only do that once you are ready.*

Most Two-Spirit people would agree with Ben's statements, and on the whole, they felt that any sort of participation in Indian communities required the acquisition of traditional knowledges. Traditional knowledges translated for some people into the basic "do's and don'ts" of Indian society, such as being respectful to elders, not drinking alcohol at Indian events, not drawing attention to oneself needlessly, and not pointing at powwows. However, individuals who were more intense viewed traditional knowledges as an understanding of Indian principles and values, historical and contemporary, which were reflected in individual social action and behavior. In this way, individual social participation and perfection of things considered traditional, such as dancing, beading, ceremony, and social obligations, sought to legitimize individuals and Two-Spirit people in general.

Often people reminded me of the role that Two-Spirit people historically held as the keepers of Native culture, and unless they perfected the performance of that culture through ceremonial knowledge and crafts, it would continue to be lost. Furthermore, learning, perfecting, and performing those knowledges helped to establish and authenticate oneself to Indian and Two-Spirit society.

— Glen: *It is our responsibility and our duty to approach the people in a good way, of course, and say, "I can do this, I can sing these songs, I can do these prayers, I know this ceremony," but when it comes down to it, we are limited in what they allow us to do.*

A lot of the young gay Indian people that come out, they have no role models. They come to the city because they want to be around other gay people and all they have is the dominant culture, their lifestyle, and their perception of what gay is. They only see the partying, the sex, going to the clubs, doing the "gay thing." When you approach them and say we're having a sweat this weekend, they hesitate, "Oh, I don't know, my white boyfriend wouldn't understand." In order to be Two-Spirit you have to realize your responsibilities and assume that role. I have a responsibility; I have to pray and I have to keep these traditions going. I have to be an example to the other Indian people. Young Indian people come to the city and they forget about their prayers.

— Ben: *The way I was taught, the men went to hunt, the women took care of the house, family, and the children, we as Two-Spirits were the ones who continued the culture: the spiritualism, the naming, the ceremonies. There was nobody else to do it. We were revered and considered as powerful people. It takes a powerful person to be able to deal with both worlds [male and female], to be spiritual for the people and conduct ceremonies. Being Two-Spirit means being very traditional, it means connecting with the tradition of the tribe.*

— Andy: *So many of the Two-Spirit people, especially those who were coming back after coming to terms with their being indigenous and gender different, really didn't know who they were. They didn't feel comfortable in their own indigenous communities. They really didn't know what their roles and responsibilities were.*

As the these statements illustrate, fulfilling traditional roles requires a significant commitment on the part of the individual. Many people not only emphasize the required connection with fulfilling one's roles, but they also emphasize Two-Spirits being active members in the creation and maintenance of communities.

Resisting Invisibility: Gay Community Awareness

"Going out to the bars" was a frequent activity when I spent time with the Colorado group. Denver as a major city had multiple thriving gay bars, restaurants, and a gay district. About two months after Sheila temporarily moved to the Oklahoma area, I took her with me on one of my research trips to Colorado so she could visit family and friends. While in Colorado we went to a local gay restaurant and to Sheila's favorite gay bar with her sister and a few other people from the Denver Society. We usually occupied the back corner of the bar, or what I came to call the Indian part of the bar. Throughout the evening, people Sheila knew were coming over to talk and catch up on her "new life" in Oklahoma. Besides the people that Sheila and the others knew, no fewer than five people came over to our area of the bar that evening and introduced themselves as Native people new to the Denver gay scene. By the end of the evening about 15 or so Indians had accumulated in the "Indian corner" battling the sound system with choruses of "Ehhhhs" and laughter. As each one of the new acquaintances left, Glen handed them a Two-Spirit Society of Denver business card with several contact numbers and e-mail addresses. When I joked with Glen about his "recruitment" of other men, he responded with the story of how he and Sheila had met in that very bar years before. Glen and Sheila both pointed out that making contacts in the gay scene was crucial for the success of the Denver Society as well as the "rescue" of other Indian men. However, they both admitted that the majority of the people they met were only interested in the social aspects of the organization and "not the commitment to a life of ceremony."

One challenge often faced by both the Oklahoma and Colorado groups is not only keeping group participants involved but also getting new people involved in Two-Spirit society. Both groups tried various means of making contact with other gay and lesbian Natives. For example, the Oklahoma group frequently ran advertisements in the local gay and Indian newspapers giving contact numbers at the clinic. Also, Ben would often go to powwows and talk to people he knew from the local gay scene but who were not involved in Two-Spirit social and religious activities. Colorado members would also use newspaper advertisements, Internet listserv announcements, and public outreach as ways to expose people to the group. Seeking out potential group members in popular gay society, such as the bar scene, while attempting to maintain a separation from popular gay society, proved to be a particularly difficult and contentious task. Efforts to find other Two-Spirit people were complicated by racism rendering Indians invisible in the gay community. Public outreach became further complicated by differing opinions on the ways to reach the invisible gay and lesbian Indians. Issues about participation in activities focused within the gay community drew many varied opinions, as did public outreach to gays and lesbians at Indian events.

Besides being present in gay bars talking to people, often Colorado group members would perform exhibition dances or sing in regalia as a part of larger cabaret or benefit shows in gay bars and gay-community-sponsored events. Some individuals saw attempts at creating gay community awareness and participation in events such as gay pride activities as giving too much to a community that had historically and continues to be hostile to them by promoting an unhealthy lifestyle for Two-Spirits and ignoring an Indian presence in outreach and politics.

Recruiting, performing, and outreach in the gay community, particularly bars, brought into question for some men whether such activities were proper Two-Spirit behavior. Wearing your regalia for demonstrations in bars where there is alcohol present, performing dance and singing exhibitions with an implied "Indians on parade" feel, and spending time supporting larger gay community organizations were understood as Two-Spirit activities with both negative and positive consequences. I was often reminded that performing in bars and having floats in gay pride parades have as their goal community awareness. Sheila, who advocates this form of outreach, pointed out that such performances create a positive image of Two-Spirits and Native gay and lesbians that may help other indigenous gays gain self- and social acceptance. The goal, according to Sheila, is "bringing more gay and lesbian Indians into the circle of Two-Spirit."

— Glen: *It can be conflictual [gay and Indian values]. People should not be around the drum if they're drunk. We've been 49ing for years; it's just a powwow and a beer bust. I am still very offended by drunks being around activities like the drum. But I realize that I have to compromise in order for us to get out into the community. In the gay community is where the people are; the people we are looking for, that's where they're at. So I have to learn to grit my teeth. We have to put up with certain things to reach the people, compromise to reach out and get the message to other Two-Spirit people. Our role as a Two-Spirit society is to reach other gay Indian people and bring them out of these destructive lifestyles. You are not going to find those people at the mall; you're gonna find them at the bar [or] on the street drunk. They are the ones that need our help.*

Sheila was proud of the many times she and Glen danced and sang during gay community benefit gatherings and conferences. In most cases these performances involved Sheila dressing in a beaded buckskin or jingle dress, and Glen in his straight dance regalia, with other people singing at a large powwow drum or hand drum. According to Sheila, these performances were directed at letting other Indian people know that one could find compatibility between their Indian identity and sexual preference. Under the pretext of awareness, these performances also had as their goal to emphasize differences within the gay community, and differences between Two-Spirit people and non-Indian gays. Sheila and Glen dressing in full regalia, singing songs in Lakota, and taking their performances seriously challenges the invisibility of Indians in the gay community. Simultaneously, these public performances, while disarticulating "gay," also provide a point of social and symbolic reference for gay Indians in the audience. Sheila often reminded me that her presence as a male-bodied person dressing in female regalia also provided a disjuncturing of popular assumptions about Indians. When seeing her dressed in female regalia, other gay Natives would recognize a complimentary relationship between being Indian and their sexual or gender orientation. She further saw performances as a way to break down anxieties that Indians have about participating in their culture, as well as the alienation they may feel in the mainstream gay community. After performances, people would frequently come up to talk to them expressing an interest in the Colorado society. When I would inquire about new members, she would tell me that they had come to the group through a connection made at one of the local gay bars.

— Sheila: *We are constantly fighting the fact that the gay community nowadays does not recognize the Two-Spirit person. When I was in Colorado, I was the "campaign queen" for the Two-Spirit group. Many of the gay organizations never heard of us, they never knew anything about Indian Two-Spirits. Indians to them are just drunks in the bars and that's all they see. They never knew there was a group, and when they found that out they picked the person who was the most traditional looking, their own personal token Sacajawea.*

While Sheila is a proponent of gaining visibility in bars, certain members of the Colorado and Oklahoma groups criticize recruiting in bars. Detractors most often cite the negative effects of the gay lifestyle, as well as the hostility toward Indians in popular gay hangouts. Andy in particular is the greatest proponent of not recruiting in bars. Simply being in a gay bar is seen as representing a negative image of Two-Spirits. Most realize the utilitarian function of gay bars as a means to find friends, sex, and relationships. However, many times I heard Andy being critical of Sheila and other people for "giving too much to the gay community." Andy, Jay, Robert, and others perceive performing in bars as equivalent to the kitschy displays of Indianness frequently found in stereotypical representations of Native Americans. When discussing others' bar performances, they would invoke the history of Indian exhibition dancing for white visitors to the reservation. In this way, many see gay bar performances as contributing to white gay community domination over Two-Spirit people, despite the assumed awareness they were intended to bring.

Using gay community events as opportunities to create awareness of indigenous gay issues could also reveal the divergence between popular gay political issues and those particular to the indigenous gay. It was common for both the GCS and Denver Society to be invited to sing at pride rallies, have floats in gay pride parades, and other activities. In 2000 people from the Denver Society and GCS traveled to the Millennium March on Washington to represent indigenous gay and lesbian issues. The Millennium March was a national gay event held in Washington DC, modeled after the Million Man March by the Nation of Islam, designed to bring awareness to gay and lesbian issues. The Denver Society brought a tipi, which they set up on the mall where the march was being held. For three days Two-Spirit men and women slept in the tipi (against march regulations), sang around the drum, and marched in their regalia. Andy was selected to represent Two-Spirit people on the podium for the rally part of the event. Andy's speech, however, generated a certain amount of controversy among the people present at the march and back in the Denver Society and GCS. As speeches go, Andy's was not unlike oratories by other peoples fighting oppression. For some of the Two-Spirit people present, the ones who saw it on television, and the others who read it via e-mail, Andy went too far in critiquing the white-dominated gay community. He made a clear and distinct link between the history of Indian–Euro-American relations and the way Two-Spirit people are treated by the gay community at large.

The awareness created by participating in gay events also made Two-Spirit men vulnerable to the lack of respect shown at times by some non-Indian gays. At the Oklahoma pride picnic the GCS had a booth where they were handing out STD literature, condoms, and other materials. The booth was an attempt at making contacts with other gay and lesbian Natives as well as creating awareness of indigenous issues in the larger gay community. Jeff and Carl brought their powwow drum to the picnic, and we spent a good portion of the day competing with the dance music on the center stage. The drum was having the intended effect of bringing other Indians over to the booth, as well as getting the attention of the gay community. Throughout the day groups of people would gather around us to listen. While the energy was mostly positive, I could not help but notice a man, who I presumed to be non-Indian, holding a can of beer dancing around beating his hand against his mouth in Wild West stereotypical fashion. He would periodically approach the booth and say "Hau Hiawatha" to Ben. Several people, including myself, were outraged by the man's mockery. Ben instead was more reflective when he pointed out, "The reason we are here in the first place is to educate gay people about who Two-Spirit people are."

The conflict over making Two-Spirit people subject to inappropriate behavior was also an issue for the Colorado group's participation in the 2001 Denver Gay Pride Parade. According to Sheila, the float for the parade was fairly simple in its design on a flatbed trailer with a raised platform where they placed an individual dressed in "regalia." Participation in the parade was already an issue of controversy, but the regalia became the point of contention for group members. The individual standing on the platform was wearing only a faux fur breach cloth and a war bonnet made of turkey feathers. Many of the Native people at the parade as well as those who participated saw this as creating a negative image of Two-Spirit people akin to an endorsement for Indian symbols as mascots. However, Sheila saw the regalia as being more easily absorbed by the mostly non-Indian gay community. She felt that if everyone dressed in their dance regalia and looked very serious, the gay community would be less likely to take notice. Sheila told me, "We were trying to make 'Indian' campy, so we would connect with those [white] queens on some level." Other Colorado group members disagreed with the motives, seeing it as not their responsibility to make Two-Spirit intelligible to the broader gay community on any other level than specifically Indian.

The Perfect Partner

In recognizing the complications that the non-Indian gay world represented, everyone acknowledged that finding another Indian partner was ideal. "I just need a traditional man" was one of Ben's most common solutions to the difficulties of having relationships with non-Indian men. For Ben and the others, non-Indian gays' lack of understanding about Native culture brought on a kind of self-imposed celibacy. Many of the older men had grown weary of having "the same relationship" every time, where they are initially sexually attracted to someone but then find the man's lack of knowledge about Indian social customs too much to overcome. While some men had long-term partnerships with non-Indian men, they were not without what Sean called "cultural problems."

During my research with the GCS Doug taught me how to bead peyote stitch.[5] For about two months I would go to his house a couple times a week to have him help me with projects. Doug was also a talented interior decorator and artist. He had completely remodeled the 1930s home where he and his non-Indian partner, Mike, lived. One evening, Doug was instructing me on how to create a bird design on a fan handle that was giving me trouble. Mike worked nights and was scarcely around when Doug and I would work on our beading projects in the evening. However, on this evening I could hear the television in the other room signaling Mike's presence. He came into Doug's studio to say hello to me, and picked up the newly made rattle Doug had proudly shown me earlier. Vigorously shaking the rattle, Mike began whooping and hopping while beating his hand against his mouth with "wow, wow, wow" sounds. Doug shot a disappointed look in my direction and told Mike to "get the hell out of here." With embarrassment Doug said, "Mike doesn't know anything about Indians and he doesn't care about my culture." Doug continued with multiple vignettes about Mike and other partners who had not understood or respected his participation in Native culture and more importantly made no effort to learn. When I asked Doug why he did not date Native men, he replied that there just were not enough gay Natives that were out of the closet. Because Doug is completely open about his sexuality, it is a requirement for his partners to be as well. He added, "You can find Indian men in the bars, but they are more absorbed in the gay lifestyle. I mean, they don't know anything about being Indians and probably don't want to be. So why not open your choices with white guys if the Indians are gonna act white anyway."

When embarking on the popular gay dating scene, Two-Spirit men see themselves at a disadvantage in several ways, namely their inability to break into a dating scene that is controlled by non-Indians who tend to be of a higher socioeconomic status. But more important were the ways non-Indian partners had the potential to misunderstand and even disrespect their ancestral heritage and cultural practices.

— Glen: *Because of my lifestyle and my work in the Two-Spirit community, my partner has to be Indian or really respect Indian ways. It would be very hard for someone who didn't understand these ways to stay in a relationship where my focus is to help Two-Spirit people. I want someone who has the same goals as I do, someone who shares my culture. I think that would keep us together.*

I've had relationships with white people who were like, 'If I hear another drum, I'm gonna scream,' or 'Honey, are you on the warpath today?' It's not their culture so it's very hard for them to understand. Even someone saying 'Columbus discovered America' can cause a fight. Columbus didn't discover America, c'mon.

A solution to Doug's, Glen's, and the other men's experiences in dating among the non-Indian gay community was finding the "perfect partner." When I asked Ben who was the perfect partner for him, he responded with the same list of qualifications that most of the other men had – traditional looking,[6] traditional in their values, does not party too much, comfortable with their sexuality, and participates in Two-Spirit society. Two-Spirit dreams of the perfect relationship included many of the things one would assume would be in a perfect relationship for any Indian couple – stability and sharing the same values and social participations. Having an Indian partner presented an alternative to the problems of having a non-Indian one but also embodied the dream of having a place for one's relationship within an Indian community. This dream could be partly realized by couples participating in Two-Spirit social activities together. However, the ultimate dream is of a couple who would be welcomed by their tribal communities and families in the same ways that their heterosexual counterparts are.

Those men who found themselves a traditional partner had to face other complications such as distance, socioeconomic status, education, and family issues. A brief relationship between Glen and Jack came to represent the Two-Spirit dream of finding the Indian ideal in a gay relationship. Glen and Jack met at a GCS gathering in early April. From that weekend through the beginning of the following spring, they became the quintessential example of the perfect partnership, and for a while Glen and Jack came to embody all our hopes for the possibilities of the perfect Two-Spirit couple. During the following eight months they went out of their way to see each other at Two-Spirit gatherings, powwows, and social events. The complications of Jack living near Eagleton and Glen living in Denver were exacerbated by both of their demanding careers, which required long and unusual work hours. In spite of the demands of distance and career, both Jack and Glen drove the ten hours to see each other. Glen met up with Jack and the rest of us at numerous powwows, and Jack would travel to Denver every couple of weeks. The commitment to newfound love was not unusual for Two-Spirit men. What made Jack and Glen unique was that both of them shared a devotion to Native spirituality, powwow dancing, and a commitment to Two-Spirit social and political goals. Jack and Glen's relationship represented the Two-Spirit men's hopes of finding an Indian partner, but it also reaffirmed that there was an alternative to the gay dating scene, an alternative that more closely resembled Two-Spirits' own social and political desires.

Despite the consistently negative experiences that men had in the gay dating scene, many of them continually returned to the bars to find companionship. This confused me somewhat, considering the dating potential among the people moving in and out of both the GCs and Denver Society. However, I was quickly corrected in my thinking by Robert, who noted, "These people are my sisters and brothers. You don't date your sisters and brothers." Ben quickly followed, "I've seen people here [GCs] hook up and date each other and it never works. It really tears the group apart when things don't work out." Sheila has seen the effects of dating within the Denver Society. Her stories about conflict over relationships in the group were almost formulaic: first, a new person comes to the group and everyone "tries to swoop in on him"; second, the new person and a group member "hook up" or start a relationship; third, they break up and one of them never returns to the society or may return only after a year or more. When I started hanging out with Sheila and the other Denver men it had been a few years since a failed relationship caused turmoil in the society. This was no doubt the result of what Sheila referred to as a "queen's agreement" for core members not to pursue newcomers for sex or relationships. She felt that "it's better for the people in leadership roles to not hit on new people. Besides, they may never come back if a bunch of people are hitting on them all the time." The limitations that Two-Spirit men put on their dating lives through rules about dating within the group as well as the search for the perfect partner created a significant amount of skepticism surrounding the potential for happiness with another man.

Jack and Glen's relationship embodied this happiness so much so that men in the GCs craved information on how things were going with them and freely shared their ideas on how to make their relationship work. People felt that Jack should move to Denver, or Glen should move to Oklahoma, that they should get married, adopt a kid, and live the "ultimate" Two-Spirit existence. Jack and Glen both seemed hopeful for the potential that their relationship held. Whenever I would talk to either of them, they were always chattering about the other and how wonderful it was to have finally "met someone." Jack was so much in love and confident about his relationship that he invited Glen to come to his tribal ceremonial dances. Nontribal members are rarely allowed to dance in the ceremonies unless one is a spouse of a tribal member.

Jack has the unique experience of being from a family that has maintained participation in their annual tribal ceremonial dances since before the reservation period in the mid-1800s. They hold positions of authority within the tribe as well as within the ceremonial community. Many of his family and tribespeople may suspect that he is gay, but because of their high profile Jack is "out" to only his mother and sister. No doubt Jack was risking further speculation about his sexuality but also potential social discredit for his family by inviting Glen. The gravity of Jack's move to be more public about his identity and Jack's mother allowing Glen to dance "under their family name" created a stir of jealousy among the men. Speculation about how Jack's family and community would react thrived in the chatter before GCS meetings were called to order. The dream of the perfect Two-Spirit relationship was coming true: traditional men caring for and respecting each other, and more importantly, a Two-Spirit couple participating in tribal culture together.

Unfortunately, the ideal of Glen and Jack began to unravel before anyone's dreams came true. An elder in Jack's tribe died the week of the ceremonial dances and out of respect for the family the celebration was canceled. Glen still came to visit Jack and was shown around the community, although in a much less conspicuous manner. Shortly after that weekend they amicably broke up. Although Glen and Jack never really spoke of any specific cause of the breakup, they both consistently pointed to distance and their careers as determining factors. Regardless of what Glen and Jack felt about their breakup, other people were devastated. Opinions on what should have been done to preserve Jack and Glen's unique relationship opportunity abounded. One GCS member criticized, "They had something you don't find everyday. I mean, two Two-Spirits who are traditional getting together. I don't think I'll ever find that." Other opinions focused more specifically on Jack and Glen's behaviors, such as being too pushy, or not understanding the other's tribal culture. Regardless of what people thought went wrong in the relationship, it serves as a reminder of the difficulties Two-Spirit men face in their pursuit of relationship happiness. Even two years after their breakup, a picture of Glen and Jack in their regalia with their foreheads touching is a cherished representation of Two-Spirit people and has been reproduced in gay magazine articles and promotional materials about Two-Spirit people.

"Healthy" Two-Spirits

Just as the perfect partner represents an alternative to the kinds of relationships available to Indians in the "white" gay community, Two-Spirit society represents a perfect way of life grounded in Native social values. Participation in activities seen as unhealthy or stereotypically gay, such as extensive use of alcohol or drugs, hanging out in the bars, having unsafe sex, or being promiscuous, were all seen specifically as not associated with Two-Spirit but more directly linked to gay society. Accordingly, unhealthy living is perceived as a personal health issue, but also one of perception. By Two-Spirit society focusing on the potential of a healthy gay lifestyle, including self-acceptance, stable relationships, and minimal substance use, they were establishing a difference between themselves and popular images of gay and lesbian culture. At one time or another, Two-Spirit people condemned most behavior seen as fulfilling mainstream non-gay society's stereotypes about same-sex desire, and popular cultural images of gay society as "flamboyant," "promiscuous," "infecting," and "risky."

There is a tension between the desire to have sex and find sex partners, and forms of behavior considered excessive and destructive. Many Two-Spirit people find themselves in a problematic situation, considering that gay bars, bathhouses, and cruising spots were some of the only places to be openly gay, find sex partners, and meet potential long-term relationship partners. Activities such as cruising in gay bars, going to places associated with gay sex, and alcohol use (both in gay contexts and in general) were seen as potentially contributing to the stereotypes that have pervaded Indian society by way of popular cultural images of gay people. Therefore, by participating in those behaviors associated with dominant perceptions of gay social/sexual practice, Two-Spirits ran the risk of being solely identified with the negative aspects of gay society by Indian communities and their peers. Furthermore, activities seen as fulfilling negative stereotypes were explicitly linked to behaviors that would lead to mental and physical illness. In most cases, ill health is perceived in terms of several intersecting factors: lack of self-esteem, alcoholism and drug abuse, and HIV infection. Individual, and thus group, survivability is explicitly compromised by having unstable relationships, HIV infection as the result of alcoholism and drug abuse or promiscuity, and mental instability as the result of self-esteem issues, which is related to all of the above. Accordingly, a healthy Two-Spirit person is one who does not behave in ways that could contribute to perceptions of a connection between Two-Spirit people and those things considered condemnable by mainstream Indian and non-Indian societies or that negate one's survivability. When I asked Mick about the link between Two-Spirit societies and healthy living, he replied, "We look at it as a more holistic thing, giving individuals a place to be who they are, to socialize away from unhealthy things like alcohol and drugs, to help build a sense of community, to help build a sense of self-esteem, so that we can basically support each other in living healthy lives." Therefore, the positioning of the Two-Spirit body within unhealthy atmospheres is seen as potentially dangerous to the person as well as the community. In this way, Two-Spirit society is often conceptualized as a healthy alternative to the negative aspects of gay society and low self-esteem. Ben and Mick comment on being healthy:

— Mick: *Unfortunately, a lot of the people, both male and female, that we would like to come to group are dealing with other issues that prevent them from wanting to come. Until they are in a place where they're ready to try and deal with those things they probably won't seek us out.*

— Brian: *Having been out to the bars with some of the guys in the group, I noticed that some people we encounter appear reluctant to come to group because they drink regularly, and are concerned about the sobriety focus. How is this a factor in participation and health issues?*

— Ben: *When we do our skills-building class, we have incorporated a lot of role playing and look at things that trigger you to do risky behaviors. People have so many issues, alcohol being one, sex addiction and drugs being another. We talk about these things and people that don't come aren't wanting to face it yet.*

— Mick: *We want to support each other in living healthy lives. Some people aren't ready to do that yet. I mean, so many people will come to gay pride when we have our booth and sit at the drum with us. I think partly shame is involved in their lack of regular participation. They fear that we are going to judge them because they have done something that is unhealthy for them. But we don't judge. I mean, there are a large number of people who are ready to stand up and try to live healthy lives that are involved with this group.*

— Ben: *I have seen our people out at the gay bars totally partying and drunk. When you have that as your number one love, you don't ever want to catch yourself too far from access to a drink. Those kinds of queens don't want to be around healthy people.*

In an effort to promote stable relationships and a positive self-image for Two-Spirit people, the Oklahoma group held what is referred to as a "skills-building workshop" on the occasional Saturday. The two all-day workshops I attended consisted of general introductions on condom use, the distribution of printed materials produced by the Centers for Disease Control and Indian Health Service, and a series of group exercises. The main focus of the workshop is the avoidance of risky behavior through self-acceptance and avoiding triggers that lead to compromising behavior. Worksheets on identifying problem behaviors or self-esteem issues were used to promote open discussion. The most revealing responses during the workshop came when people divulged various experiences in which they felt they had compromised their health by consuming too much alcohol or participating in unprotected sex, as well as negative aspects about their romantic relationships. These discussions took the form of a talking circle, where an eagle feather is passed from person to person and they responded to questions asked by Mick or Ben. Responses generally addressed the ways in which people were reflecting on behaviors that compromised their relationships or health. However, the overriding theme involved individuals using their identity as Two-Spirit as a resource to overcome unhealthy aspects of their behavior, negative relationships, or self-esteem issues. Most people in the talking circle stated that once they had emphasized the Native aspects of their identity, they had more positive feelings about being gay. They felt that identifying as Two-Spirit allowed them to build their self-confidence and focus their attention on what many characterized as the "more positive aspects of being gay and Indian."

There is an ebb and flow of individuals in and out of Two-Spirit social activities, reflecting the tension between Two-Spirit society as healthy and the gay community as harmful. It was assumed that when someone's participation in Two-Spirit activities dropped off, they had "gone back to the bars." Going back to the bars is seen as an explicit choice to prefer drinking and promiscuity over the self-control required to participate in Two-Spirit activities. But it is also seen as a choice to turn specifically from the spirituality of Two-Spiritedness. Accordingly, a common theme in distinguishing Two-Spirit from the perceptibly negative gay social realm is the path to "getting healthy." Ben often told me that he felt he was living unhealthily when he first came out and was going to the bars. Unhealthy living for Ben was drinking excessively, doing drugs, and having sex with random people at bathhouses and cruising spots, all of which he and others readily associated with mainstream gay society.

— Ben: *We are all here on earth trying to find who we connect to and what our purpose is in life. I feel like that when I became connected spiritually [Two-Spirited], I started on that journey. When I first came out I partied. I was a heavy drinker, heavy drug user. I was still searching and I just went off the path. We start blocking out those parts of our lives [gayness, Indianness] because we think it is wrong. We get so far off the path that we start trying to find it in alcohol, drugs, whatever we can find to fill that void. When I was going out to gay bars and getting drunk I was still on my journey. I just had to learn that the two don't mix [journey and alcohol].*

I was in major denial about my gayness. I grew up in a mostly non-Indian world. My dad was a minister. They made me feel ashamed. I didn't want to be Indian, because I wanted to fit in. I was running from

*everything: my gayness, my Indianness. You see, once I started on my jour-
ney as a Two-Spirit person I became healthy.*

The bad habits of popular gay society also drove Andy to seek refuge in
his Native identity.

— *Andy: I came out and immersed myself in gay culture. I moved to* LA,
*went out to the bars, and did that whole scene. But there was always some
component of it, some element of it that didn't fit. It was fine but it was a
culture surrounded around sex, especially gay male culture. It left out the
other elements that were part of who I am, the Indian and the gay elements that never communicated with one another.*

*I stumbled across this Two-Spirit community at a major gay event in
Washington and I figured out that I was not the only one who feels this
way. I was already doing work in the Colorado community, but it was HIV
work for gays, not Two-Spirit. The work I was doing didn't make me feel
any better because I was experiencing the same racism and discrimination
in the gay community that I was experiencing in the general white community. I also needed that spiritual connection only found in the Indian
traditions.*

Real Two-Spirits

Despite the ways Two-Spirit society offered an alternative to the gay
scene, the sheer number of Indian people I knew from local communities, powwows, and ceremonies who I then saw in gay bars was surprising to me. I was further surprised when those people involved in Indian
communities and the gay community separately, vehemently declined
to participate in Two-Spirit society and social activities. Mick, Ben, and
I had a discussion about this issue, where I became somewhat of an
informant.

— *Brian: The other night I was out with some of my friends and there was
a whole group of gay Indians that I had seen out with Sheila before. I
started talking to them, and one of them said, "You aren't gonna start talking about that damn group [Two-Spirit] again are you?" Mick, what do
you attribute to that attitude?*

— Mick: *They may have had a negative experience in the group or with group members before. They may be in denial about having HIV or their risks for that. It could be the alcohol thing. I mean, for my information, when you were talking to them, did you get an inkling of why they didn't want to participate?*

— Brian: *One guy, I think he is Choctaw. For him the issue was being "out." There were also some Comanche people who said they had never been around the Indian community. They said that they had grown up in Arizona, and gay people thought they were Mexican, and that was just fine with them. In some way, they seemed not to care about being identified as Indian by other people.*

— Mick: *So they don't have any connection with their Indianness?*

— Brian: *Right. That's the idea I got from them. To an extent, some of them appeared to be worried about the real Indian thing. You know, being judged about not knowing anything and the way they look or act.*

In addition to the dilemmas that Two-Spirit men face in locating a place for themselves in the gay community, they also attempt to negotiate a place within Two-Spirit society. This negotiation involves managing the complications of contemporary Native identity politics. At any one time Two-Spirit societies include people who grew up in families immersed in traditional tribal culture, men whose first experience with Indian culture is in the Two-Spirit society, men who grew up Christian and were taught that Native traditional practices were satanic, and those people whose claims of Indian identity draw suspicion from other members of the Two-Spirit community. Two-Spirit society also includes people who are of a high blood quantum and "look Indian" but know very little about Native cultural practices. As often as I heard individuals detail the social, sexual, and spiritual requirements of being Two-Spirit, I heard people readily dismiss individuals identifying as Two-Spirit based on how they looked, whether they were enrolled in a tribe, and if the tribe required a high or low blood quantum, whether they participated in their tribal culture, and if their upbringing, behavior, and knowledge were characterized as traditional. Under these criteria, recognition of Two-Spirit identity became indistinguishable from the criteria an individual would have to meet to be legitimately considered Indian by most mainstream and tribal community standards.[7] Many individuals showed a disdain for racial ideologies such as "Indian pedigrees" (blood quantum). But for the most part I witnessed, and experienced firsthand, the exacting privilege maintained by those individuals who were characterized as phenotypically traditional looking, grew up on "the rez," or had politically and socially powerful families in the Indian community. The dispensation that certain individuals experienced is almost exclusively a result of their adherence to dominant standards, Indian and non-Indian, about who is the ideal type of person to be called Indian. Inevitably, individuals are subject to the discourse on Indian identity as a means to determine who is legitimately Two-Spirit and Indian as well as who is not. Individuals become subjects of questions of authenticity, public and private, often grounded in the semiotic markers between such socially recognized identities as Two-Spirit, gay, Indian, and white. Accordingly, it is within the dialectic of Indian, gay, and Two-Spirit where identity is figured, translated, and acted out, resulting in a set of exclusionary and inclusive features based on notions of cultural and racial authenticity.

Phillip Deloria's study of "Indian play" discusses the intersection of race and cultural practice where individuals who "imagined an accessible Indian culture, also refigured racial difference around at least three variables – genetic quantum, geographical residence, and cultural attitude. The highest possible degree of authenticity inhered in the traditional, reservation-based full blood. The least authentic figure was the progressive, urban, low-quantum mixed-blood" (1998:143). The "commingling of racial essentialism with the behavior that helped define a culture," as Deloria points out, complicates perceptions of the authentic, thereby making all behavior, attitudes, appearance, and practice subject to racialization (1998:143). Changing ideas about authenticity through time have exacerbated Two-Spirit alienation. That is, as the Indian societies came to question the social status of the gender different over the last five centuries, the gender different became an unrecognizable part of many tribal cultures. Combining this form of alienation with the myriad of ways "Indianness" can be defined by social characteristics, cultural participation, and tribal enrollment further complicates definitions of what Two-Spirit is and who can legitimately claim it as an identity. People's dominant notions of authenticity led to their dividing Two-Spiritedness into the ways it could be behaviorally and physically manifested in signs and symbols. As we have seen with the conceptual differences between gay and Two-Spirit, Two-Spirit people have used dominant ideas on what constitutes authentically Indian, and thus authentically Two-Spirit. Two-Spirit men's attempts to sort out the influence of gay culture on Two-Spiritedness are matched by their efforts to negotiate the politics of being Indian.

Most of the men I interviewed and interacted with showed disdain for the use of blood quantum, tribal enrollment, and someone's appearance as criteria for accepting people into Two-Spirit society. The disturbing and destructive nature of racial essentialism in Indian society came up frequently in everyday conversations and interviews. Yet some Two-Spirit people readily employed essentialist ideals when discerning who had the right to call themselves Indian and thus Two-Spirit. One of the most telling sources of the various opinions was the yearlong debate over the criteria required to gain access to a Two-Spirit web post, which ironically turned into a debate over what characteristics a person should possess to be considered a "real" Two-Spirit.

When establishing the gay and lesbian Indian e-mail post group, Juan, the creator and manager of the group, was grappling with the issue of who should be allowed to join the group conversation and be able to view some of the personal information being disseminated by e-mail. To determine who could get access, Juan posed the question, "Does appearance, cultural practices, knowledge of tribal customs, etc., impact your decision about who is Two-Spirit?" For over a year this single question created a sometimes fierce dialogue directly addressing the issue of blood- and community-derived identity. Immediately, group members seized the opportunity to make their views on Two-Spirit identity known, which inevitably included opinions on race, blood quantum, and cultural participation:

— Simon: *My point is that the shared perspectives and values are more likely to be common ground for those whose quantum is one quarter or more. I really don't care if one is enrolled or not. . . . I am more interested in the socialization aspects and the nondilution of our voices. One example is the fact that a person who is 1/64th (or less) Indian can be an enrolled member of the Cherokee tribe. Now, am I to believe this person is likely to have our shared values and should automatically be part of this group? Don't think so. If this person ever has a nosebleed, (s)he will be in deep shit.*

— Chance: *What you are asking us to define is, Who is Native? An easy way is, of course, enrollment. But how accurate is this? Does this mean that those individuals who are not enrolled are not, in fact, Native simply because they are not eligible for benefits?*

Practice of culture is not necessarily an indicator either. Many of us know people who are full blood and do not identify with their heritage at all. There are also people who, like myself, are mixed blood and quite light, who are vested in their culture and those practices. I believe that we need to try very hard to not exclude those who may not be able to document their lineage but believe themselves to be two-spirited.

— Paul: *This is a very emotional issue for groups of our culture to address. In my tribe, acceptance was granted for many diverse groups of people, not only those born into the tribe. Persons who had proven themselves to be worthy of tribal acceptance ranged from white, black, Hispanic, and other Indian tribes. Acceptance did not mean specifically tribal membership, although some were granted this privilege, but all were allowed to live and participate freely with the tribal consigns. As for myself, I am enrolled but I also have to stop and consider what that specifically means. Blood quantum to me is a term that was invented by the white government as a means to insure all the subdued (a polite term) Indian nations [were] recorded on the rolls of the Bureau of Indian Affairs–approved registry.*

In making the unambiguous connection between individual definitions of what it means to be Two-Spirit and mainstream conceptions about blood and cultural Indianness in contemporary society, Two-

Spirit men readily applied dominant community standards about authenticity to themselves and one another. As opinions vary from those who saw Indian identity based on blood and those who saw it embedded in community participation and recognition, they reveal ways in which ongoing debates in tribal communities are reflected in Two-Spirit ideas of identity.

Considering that more than three quarters of the Two-Spirit people I knew would identify as mixed blood, it is not surprising that many of them showed tremendous contempt for blood quantum as an indicator of Two-Spiritedness or as a prerequisite for individuals to participate in Two-Spirit society.

— Andy: *I have worked very hard in my life to cast off all vestiges of colonialism. I am a mixed blood and I know very well who I am and have no doubts about how "Indian" I am. What I have experienced, however, even within the indigenous communities, are forms of racism so deep-seated they could only have come from teachings of the white man. There is, at times, righteousness with those that have been registered that I lose all hope for there ever being a return to the "place of harmony" that our ancestors knew.*

— Glen: *Attitudes are there where people say, "Who is he to tell me something 'cause he's mixed blood?" I can see why people are suspicious of mixed bloods because of the wannabe thing, and when people meet me I can tell they are a little standoffish.*

Mick, as a mixed blood, was particularly vulnerable to the onslaught of racial politics. Mick could trace his ancestry through the Cherokee and Lumbee tribes and African American slaves. However, Mick's complexion and physical features did not reveal this ancestry. As a blond-haired, blue-eyed man of light complexion, Mick was well aware of the doubt his claims to Native ancestry created. Because Mick's family was not involved in any Indian communities and did not emphasize that aspect of their heritage, he could not draw on the cultural capital that family connections or cultural knowledge often provide. Mick continuously updated Ben and me on the status of his getting an enrollment card from the Lumbees, as not having a relative on the proper Cherokee roll made the Lumbees his only option for citizenship in a nation. A tribal membership card was the only conceivable way to "prove" his ancestry to other Indians, considering his lack of features endorsed by society as stereotypically Indian. For Mick, being accepted by other Indians was twofold. He wanted to be accepted as Native by the larger Indian community, but also by other Two-Spirit people.

As one of the leaders of the GCS, Mick was in a vulnerable position for racial criticism. Mick was in charge of HIV community outreach for the clinic and often traveled to tribal headquarters and Indian Health Service clinics around Oklahoma, Kansas, Arkansas, and Texas to conduct presentations on HIV and gay and lesbian issues. From the very beginning the communities were reluctant to grant Mick the status of "Indian," which further complicated his mission of informing others about the threat of HIV to Indian people. Mick felt that being open about his sexuality combined with his lack of Indian features compounded his lack of legitimacy for other Indian peoples. Indian people's initial responses to Mick's presentations on Native gender diversity and HIV were almost formulaic. Besides questioning the acceptance of same-sex relations in historic Native America, people would question Mick's authority as a "white person" on Indian sexuality and health matters. When Mick asserted his ancestral background to the participants, it only increased their doubt and put him into the category of wannabe. Mick commented on people's reactions: "Over the years people have grown to be more accepting of me, because they see me being respectful and acting in a good way. But there will always be people that doubt my Indianness."

Mick experienced doubt not only from the Oklahoma Indian community at large but also from other Two-Spirit men. Mick's commitment to the cause of HIV prevention, treatment, and social rights for the infected helped legitimize his leadership role in the GCS. Yet people were reluctant to see him as an authority on Native cultural practices. In the last six months of Mick's time as director of the GCS, a large number of new members joined the group. Among the new members were a group of men who were recognizably Native and knowledgeable about their tribal culture. Unlike longtime members of the GCS, they were more publicly vocal about issues of racial and cultural authenticity. Shortly after the arrival of the new men, Mick resigned his position at the clinic to become the director of a nonprofit agency. At Mick's farewell party, some of the men voiced their opinions about his claim to Indianness. When Ben asked us to tell a way Mick had touched our lives, most of the men told funny stories about their experiences with Mick or how he had inspired them. When it was Neal's turn, he said, "When I first met Mick, I thought, 'Wow he's hot, but Indian, no way!'" Neal's comment opened the door for other men to proclaim their doubt about Mick's Indianness. It was not long before Mick made a quick and irritated exit. Six months later I saw Mick and asked him about that night, to which he replied, "At my new job I don't have to care about race anymore. I know who I am and no one asks me to prove it."

Mick was well liked among the GCS but the men turned to Ben when they needed some advice or knowledge about Indian social or cultural practices. Ben is by popular standards more Indian looking because he has dark skin, dark eyes, and wears his black hair in braids. Ben frequently wore multiple pieces of turquoise jewelry and dressed in the style of the Western Indian. Ben also has extensive contacts in the Indian community and is privy to gossip about tribal and urban Indian politics. GCS group members repeatedly referred to Ben as being "more Indian" than Mick, no doubt a result of his looks and cultural knowledge. When I asked a few people why it was important to make this distinction, they felt that Ben had experienced more of the same kinds of discrimination that they had. But they also felt that having Ben as a leader made the GCS look like "we are real Indians" and that "other Indians [gay and non-gay] would be less suspicious of us and we will be taken more seriously if we all don't look like a bunch of white people pretending to be Indian." Feeling as if their fellow Two-Spirits shared their racial experiences was an important aspect of building a community, but presenting their best possible face to seem "real" was also important.

Dale told me multiple times that he should be the leader of a Two-Spirit society, because he was the "only full blood in the group." Dale was in fact registered with his tribe as a full blood, and had all of the physical features that would make him recognizably Native. Having a "real Indian" as the leader and the person who would represent the Two-Spirit society to other people was important for the legitimacy it would give to the organization. Dale assumed that new members at a Two-Spirit group meeting would be more likely to continue to participate if the other members looked phenotypically Indian and behaved in recognizably Indian ways. A real Indian not only would be more recognizable by the non-Indian gay community, and therefore more likely to be believed, but also could further legitimize Two-Spirit as a racially authentic identity to other Native people. The fear was that other Indians would see Two-Spirit people as a group of wannabe Indians or New Age lesbigays. What prevented Dale's rise to a leadership role in a Two-Spirit community was his lack of knowledge about his tribal practices as well as common Native cultural practices. That is, Dale's lack of cultural knowledge did not match the assumptions generated by his physical features. Upon meeting Dale, most people assumed that he was a full blood who had grown up on a reservation in a decidedly traditional family. However, Dale was what the men referred to as a "city Indian," in that he grew up in a city or town without access to his tribal religion or participating in powwows. By not knowing much of his tribal culture, Dale's racial assertions were somewhat turned on their head. Ironically though, Dale enjoyed an authenticity unavailable to the less Indian looking but more knowledgeable men.

Initially I was alarmed by the ways Two-Spirit men used racial determinism to delineate who was a real Two-Spirit and who was not. Yet again, Sean forcefully reminded me, "Brian, you act like we are not Indians. I mean we [Indians] use the way someone looks to figure out whether someone is Indian or not all the time. Just because we are gay we're supposed to accept everyone who comes through the door? My tribe isn't gonna do that, so why would I?"

Two-Spirits and "New Age Lesbigays"

Even though they employ racial determinism in their discernment of identity, Two-Spirit men are by and large more accepting of people who are not phenotypically Indian looking or enrolled in a specific tribe than are the majority of tribal communities. As a result of their compound alienation as gay and Indian, Two-Spirit men felt that they needed to be more welcoming to other people, otherwise they risk reinforcing the kinds of discrimination they are fighting against. This cautious welcoming of new people has made Two-Spirit societies a route for non-Indian New Age lesbigays to gain access to Native ceremonial and social practices.[8] Like Two-Spirit men, the New Age lesbigays feel alienated from more mainstream religions and other social outlets. They, too, face the quandary of either hiding their sexual orientation to be more acceptable to their families and communities, or being out and attempting to locate social circles where they are welcome. The desire to find a place where they are welcome, combined with the romanticization of Native cultural practices within the New Age religious and neo-hippie movement, motivates many non-Indian lesbigays to answer Two-Spirit societies' ads in gay newspapers and posters hung in bars. Some Two-Spirit men have come to see them as permanent fixtures who can contribute to the overall cause, whereas others see them as a constant annoyance that diverts the social and political goals of the group back into white stereotypes of Indians.

One incident has come to define the ways Two-Spirit people see New Age lesbigays. Glen, Matt, and Jeff were putting up a tipi for meetings and ceremonies at the campsite of the Denver Society gathering. A few other people were helping out by holding onto lodge poles. Glen was clearing rocks and twigs from the tipi site. A little pine sapling was in the way of one of the poles, and Glen jerked it out of the ground, roots and all, tossing it into the brush. Immediately a girl I did not know moaned, holding her chest, and said, "Oh God, I felt that." We all started cracking up; we honestly thought she was joking. But she was dead serious, as we quickly learned, and very upset at Glen's lack of respect for nature, reminding everyone "such disrespect was not the Indian way." News of this "freakish" and "granola" behavior spread through the camp rapidly, particularly the men's camp, and soon became a running joke. This incident has become a notorious example of "wannabe behavior" among the Two-Spirit witnesses, and years later is often told anecdotally. The group's opinion of the girl's status as a wannabe or "New Age granola" was exacerbated by her lightness of complexion and her not being enrolled in a tribe or knowing much of everyday Native culture. But it was the "New Agey" things she said and did that solidified others' impressions of her.

Not long after my first research trip to Colorado, I realized that the Denver Society drew considerable interest from Boulder-based New Age lesbigays. "New Age lesbigay" is a phrase often applied to gays and lesbians who are seeking a form of spiritual participation through the socially liberal New Age religious movement, which focuses on a syncretism of non-Western traditions, particularly ancient Egyptian, Native American, Hindu, and Buddhist. For gays and lesbians, this movement emphasizes spiritual fulfillment outside the largely homophobic Christian religion. The Two-Spirit men mostly referred to the non-Native New Age lesbigays as "granolas" and "New Age wannabes." The Denver group's spiritual focus and proximity to large pockets of New Age liberals made them particularly susceptible to lesbigay spiritual interests. Denver, Boulder, and surrounding communities are widely known to have a significant population of social liberals. The result is that many students and young professionals are seeking enrichment from non-Western cultural and religious ideas. Organizations such as the Naropa Institute in Boulder make Hinduism, Buddhism, and Native religious practices available to the general public. The interest in and availability of non-Western religions has led New Age lesbigays to see participation in Two-Spirit organizations as another form of personal and social fulfillment. Accordingly, there are a significant number of people who attempt to involve themselves in Two-Spirit society who have vague Indian ancestry and little or no experience with everyday ways of being Indian. Two-Spirit men had strong feelings about non-Indian gays' co-opting of Native traditions.

— Burt: *My own belief is that [allowing non-Indians to participate] would be a great disservice to the group. Wouldn't you agree that everything else about Indians has already undergone cultural appropriation by*

123

outsiders? I do sympathize with outsiders who have no heritage that allows or dignifies their existence.

— Jim: *I also believe that we need to exclude those who are simply curious. Through colonization and Western religion, many of us have developed a negative image of who and what we are. This is a place to become more comfortable with ourselves and with those who are like us in a setting of privacy and community without the ever-present voyeurism that follows Native people in the world at large.*

— Andy: *For both the gathering and the listserv out of the Bay Area, the solution was simple. Ask the individual if they are Indian, what relationship they have with their community, what do they call themselves, and why they want to join. In my experience, if a person does not belong, you will know it and can politely decline their request.*

— Zach: *I personally have mixed feelings about non-Indians becoming involved with Native ways. We are taught to accept who comes, that they are supposed to be a part of what happens, but there are also many who want a spiritual vacation, or have been Native in a past life and feel that they should be accepted. I loathe having to educate these individuals and would prefer that they go to receive their training from those persons who have been given the gift to teach these things. There are too many people who want a quick fix of the Native spiritual way of life.*

Suspicions about non-Indian lesbigays fuel an intense scrutiny of new participants whose motives and claims to Indianness appear questionable. The first thing newcomers to a Two-Spirit society notice is the onslaught of questions about where they are from and who are their people – what Sheila refers to as the "Indian test." Zach explains, "I do have to be honest in saying that when someone approaches me about being Indian, I do have certain criteria that I go by. I want to know where they grew up and if it was on a rez, and if they grew up with some sort of connection to their spirituality." Frequently, New Age lesbigays lack the kinds of knowledge one would expect them to have if they were Indian, namely their tribal affiliation. New Age neophytes who were questioned about their tribal ancestry "seemed to pull a tribe out of the air" or told of a "long-held secret of Indian ancestry" in their family. At the first Two-Spirit meeting I attended, I immediately noticed that when we went around the room to introduce ourselves, everyone said their name and their tribal affiliation. In this way, new individuals are often publicly put on the spot. If others share that affiliation, they would ask the newcomers about their family names to see if they were related and no doubt test their claims. Individuals who did not have believable connections with a tribe or basic knowledge of Indian social customs, such as humor, drew the suspicion of other Two-Spirit people. Native societies in general rely on an individual's ability to express the legitimacy of their claims through associations with specific tribal communities or customs. These "Indian tests" serve as a way not only to get a sense of another person's experiences but also to ascertain someone's motives for participating in Two-Spirit society.

Two-Spirit men are politely welcoming, but at the same time, the presence of New Age lesbigays created a considerable amount of conflict among people in the Denver group. The conflict lay in how the men viewed the role of newcomers, who may be Indians with little cultural knowledge, New Age lesbigays with suspect claims to Indianness, and non-Indian gays desiring a connection to Native cultural practices. Some Two-Spirit men see the welcoming of non-Indians and New Age lesbigays as an act of true traditionalism, in the spirit of the practice of adopting people from other tribes or non-Indians into one's community. Others see the influence of non-Indians as diffusing Two-Spirit society's focus on the issues faced by gay and lesbian Natives. Two-Spirit men who had direct knowledge of their culture, had grown up in Indian communities or on reservations, and maintained participation in Native social practices were often the most put off by the presence of New Age lesbigays. However, Two-Spirit men who did not have access to their tribal ceremonies and those who were not exposed to their tribal religious practices as children were also drawn to New Age interpretations of Native religious practices. Those New Agers who were recognizably Indian or enrolled were often given more opportunities to gain the trust of the other men. They were at least seen as having had some of the same racial and political experiences of other Natives.

I became acutely aware of the conflict over New Agers at the Denver Society gathering. As Robert and I walked up the hill to the camp, Jack greeted us with "Finally some real Indians are here." (I took my inclusion into "real Indians" as more a sign of courtesy than anything else.) It was day six of the ten-day gathering, and clashes over the New Agers threatened to tear the camp apart. This gathering drew a larger number of people than in years before. Publicity through various gay media sources and word of mouth had brought almost 100 gays, lesbians, and some of their non-Indian partners to the camp from around the United States and Canada. Unlike the male-focused GCS gathering, the Denver group included Native lesbians in their annual gathering, as their participation was considered important to the indigenous gay rights cause. Despite the effort at inclusion, there was an inevitable division between the women and men at the camp. The women viewed the men as adhering far too rigidly to the gender structure of contemporary Native society, especially when it came to sweat lodges. The sweat lodge, as it is practiced as a general ceremony in popular Native culture, has a taboo against the participation of women "who are on their moon" (menstruating), especially in "mixed lodges" of men and women. The taboo restricting ceremonial access for women during their menses is fairly common in multiple tribal societies.[9] The issue of having menstruating women in the sweat lodges held twice a day caused significant controversy, so much so that a "council meeting" had to be called to put the issue before gathering attendees. The men saw adhering to such taboos as a traditional necessity. To make matters worse, Jacob's father, who had traveled from Arizona as a spiritual advisor, would not perform mixed lodges. The women argued that if Two-Spirit people are in fact of both male and female spirits, then the gender rules concerning ceremonies should not apply, especially in a Two-Spirit context. The women took the men's insistence on menstruation taboos as a sign of their reinforcing the gender hierarchy that they all were attempting to challenge. The result of these disagreements led to a division of the camp into the "lesbian camp" and those men that sided with them, and the "men's camp" and the women who sided with them.

The division in the camp had less to do with gender than with divisions over those "who knew" and who did not. That is, the women's camp became associated with those people who did not have the appropriate kinds of knowledge to be included in the symbolic parameters of the "knowing." The people recognized as the "knowing" were largely made up of the men and women who had grown up on reservations or in culturally active urban communities. They were also the people who often led ceremonies such as sweat lodges. The men's camp came to view itself as a haven of cultural certainty. Inevitably, the women began having their own sweat lodges that included those women who were on their moon. The effect of this division eventually led to my not being able to talk with many of the Two-Spirit women, seeing as I am a male and a "friend of the men's camp." The tension was finally broken at the giveaway on the final day of camp when Andy gave the women's camp leader, Ida, his eagle-wing fan.

The ill feelings over gender rules were exacerbated by the men's belief that most of the New Agers were "colonizing" the Two-Spirit camp. No more than 15 minutes after my arrival, Sheila and Jack were updating me on the "wannabe behaviors" of the "New Age granolas." One of the first stories I heard was about a "possessed" hand drum. A few people were hanging around the fire singing, as was the practice after dinner, when a man became distraught and threw his hand drum into the campfire, claiming "it was filled with demon spirits." When telling the story, Zach joked, "What kind of Indian throws a perfectly good hand drum into a fire?" Eagerness to make one's intensity of spirituality or "medicine" known to others is something that divided the New Agers from the men who identified themselves as the "real Indians." Being a "real Indian" did not reside only in one's knowledge of ceremonial practices. As Sheila mocked, "Let's face it. Most of the stuff you need to know about having a sweat lodge, you can find in books by anthropologists. These people have to have a ceremony every time a tree falls or a pigeon feather hits the ground." Sean saw a contradiction in the New Agers' intense interest in Native culture: "What's puzzling to me is, why are these vegetarians so interested in a culture based on the exploitation of animals? I mean, everything from the traditional foods we eat to our regalia is based on animals. Indians respected nature, yes. But we were also very violent people who had to do severe things to live in our world. So I think it's odd that those guys [New Agers] admire us so much."

By demanding vegetarian meals at camps and eating natural foods, insisting on natural soaps, dressing in Birkenstock sandals and other clothes associated with New Age hippies, and wearing "shaman bags" with crystals in them around their necks, many people solidified their New Age wannabe status. The men's camp balked at these idealized visions of the "naturalness" of Native spirituality and culture. More important, however, than food choice or clothes was the fact that many of the people marked as New Age wannabes were seen as displaying a narcissistic view of their own spirituality, which is not considered a noble value among most Native people. Sheila came to make fun of people who had what she called "medicine man syndrome," referring to the New Age idea that everyone has the ability to become a medicine person, and it is up to the individual to claim his or her own spiritual power or "medicine" by whatever means necessary. In most tribal cultures individuals gain their right to perform ceremonies through a series of interactions with the spirit world, through which they receive a "calling." Fulfilling the rights and responsibilities of their vocation is then obtained through the process of learning under the tutelage of someone "who knows." Besides the sacrifices involved in learning the required knowledge and living a life in service of the people, they also must have the approval of their tribal society to effectively perform ceremonies. That is, they must be recognized by their fellow tribespeople as having the proper knowledge and abilities.

However, for the New Agers, becoming a "medicine person" was merely a process of studying and learning by whatever means available, whether from a guidebook or a long weekend at a seminar. Most of the people recognized as New Age lesbigays insisted on their being Indian, yet they lacked access to the tribal connections necessary to obtain community-sanctioned knowledge or the performance of ceremonies. Rather, much of their knowledge comes from books on Native religion, instructional classes on performing ceremonies, and to the chagrin of many tribal peoples, from medicine men seeking financial gain. On the whole, they are instructed in Plains-style religious practices, particularly the Seven Rites of the Lakota, also known as the Pipe Religion. Through their studies they learn to perform sweat lodges, say prayers in Lakota, conduct pipe ceremonies, and perform parts of the Sun Dance and vision quests. Many times they will supplement these ceremonies with other religious philosophies, mostly Eastern ones such as Buddhism. Some of the New Age lesbigays, though recognized as having ambiguous claims to Native ancestry, were quite knowledgeable about tribal customs. In some cases they were recognized as having more knowledge about ceremonial practices than people actually from that tribe.

Despite their proficiency in Native culture, New Age lesbigays represent a contradiction for many of the people who not only grew up attending ceremonies among their own tribes but also "grew up Indian." The men frequently reminded me that being Indian and Two-Spirit was about more than one's participation in ceremonialism. Being a Two-Spirit man was also about one's experiences as an Indian person, which not only included being a member of a community with connections to historical societies and cultural practices but also experiencing the disadvantages that go with being different in America. They saw the New Agers as coming from a position of privilege and as completely lacking in the class experiences caused by racism and ethnocentrism. That is, Two-Spirit men assumed the New Age wannabes' lack of outward signs of Indianness, such as dark skin or historic surnames like Four Arrows, had given them certain socioeconomic advantages. The men were confused as to why the New Age wannabes mobilized this privilege to supposedly choose their own race. It was then puzzling that they were either lying about having Indian ancestry or exaggerating it simply to gain access to Two-Spirit social activities. In one alcohol-infused conversation, Zach worked himself into a frenzy and asked me if I thought "these wannabes were going to go to the reservation and start living in shit holes, with no job and eat commodities?" I replied with a firm "probably not."

Nonparticipant Viewers

Overeager New Age wannabes are countered by another category of persons, which Ben referred to as the "nonparticipant viewers." Nonparticipant viewers are Two-Spirit men of Native ancestry who might look Native and are enrolled or have explicit ties to a tribe but have no significant knowledge of or participation in their tribal culture or knowledge of popular Indian culture such as powwows. These men are involved in Two-Spirit organizations but seek to draw different benefits from the experience. The nonparticipant viewer is defined by his tendency to observe but show no interest in being culturally Indian. That is, these men would sit for hours watching powwows or stomp dances but would decline to participate. They had no desire to learn to bead, did not wear Native jewelry, and did not wish to participate in any kind of singing or ceremonies. According to Ben, the absence of interest in cultural knowledge is the result of several factors for these Two-Spirit men. First, they grew up feeling ashamed of their sexual orientation and as a result alienated themselves from tribal social life. Second, they had a family that completely turned away from Native cultural practices for social and religious reasons. And third, they were raised at a geographic distance from their tribal community. Ben saw that the men's lack of contact with tribal or popular Indian customs throughout their lives had created "an entire generation of Two-Spirit men with no idea what it means to be an Indian." Nonparticipants had indeed experienced what it was like to be recognizably Indian by name, looks, and enrollment, but lacked the kinds of experiences that would give them the knowledge to understand Indian humor or know specifics of their tribal social customs.

By Ben's definition, the GCS had the largest number of nonparticipant viewers, and these men shared similar backgrounds. Most were brought up in intensely Christian homes, most were in the closet (some were even married), and many bore a marker that tied them to Native or tribal identity, such as appearance, surname, or tribal enrollment. Despite self-identifying as Native, their lack of knowledge of historic tribal culture or popular Indian culture created difficulties for the men.

Other GCS members would often associate the nonparticipants' markers of Indianness with cultural authority, particularly with what is defined as "traditionalism." Traditionalism in popular Native society basically refers to the social and cultural practices seen as having the closest connection to precontact Native culture. According to this logic, a Lakota who practices the Pipe Religion would be considered traditional, whereas a Catholic Lakota would not. For example, in the beginning of my research, I often made the mistake of assuming that someone who identified as Creek and lived in the geographic region where Creeks were concentrated had experiences with Creek Stomp Dance practices. My misstep was met with the statement, "We are Church people," meaning that their family was Christian and involved with an Indian Christian church. Other times individuals gave sociohistoric reasons, such as "My family are all city Indians," for their own or their family's lack of knowledge of traditionalism or lack of participation in certain practices. As a result of their Christian and urban upbringing, most nonparticipants had little desire to take part in the non-Christian rituals of traditionalism, such as smudging or singing at the drum. Ben and Mick made numerous attempts to teach GCS members how to sing at the drum, learn tribally specific practices such as the Stomp Dance, or help them put together their powwow regalia. Most of these attempts were met with a burst of enthusiasm that quickly petered out or were resisted by a total lack of interest. GCS meetings that focused on learning a traditional practice, such as singing or beading, were often met with a lack of enthusiasm and poor attendance. As Ben pointed out in frustration, "Many of these queens are scared of traditional culture because they were programmed to be ashamed of being gay as well as being Indian."

What troubled culturally active Two-Spirit men about the nonparticipant viewers was the disconnect they represented between being an Indian and the kinds of social and cultural practices everyone felt should embody Two-Spirit identity. The nonparticipant lacked the kinds of behavioral attributes and social participations that symbolize contemporary Indian and tribal identity. As we have seen, Two-Spirit men distinctly believe that participating in Native social and ceremonial culture is a crucial aspect of Two-Spirit identity. Nonparticipant viewers, however, showed little interest in incorporating ceremonial knowledge and practice into their lives. It was assumed that these men cared little about being Native and cared more about being gay. Yet others more thoughtfully characterized nonparticipants as individuals who chose to limit their participation in ceremonial activities deemed Indian for religious reasons, or people who had yet to become comfortable with bringing their sexuality and racial identity into their notion of self. Many men could not fathom why an individual who readily identified himself as Indian would not be interested in participating in Native ceremonial and social activities. As a counselor of Native men, Ben was well aware that many of these men were simply scared to participate. They were scared that they would embarrass themselves, that other Indians would make fun of them for doing something wrong, or they had made a negative association between the heteronormative aspect of Indian culture and their own sexuality and gender identity. Ben saw the nonparticipant viewer as yet another example of the ways Two-Spirit men have difficulty finding a place for themselves.

Ben inevitably placed the responsibility for gay Native men's difficulties in finding a place for themselves squarely on the shoulders of tribal communities: "What are our people [Two-Spirit] supposed to do? These queens don't know anything because they were never given the chance, and now they want to get back into their culture but are afraid. They are afraid of the people that are supposed to be their relations."

CHAPTER FIVE

Cultural Compromise at Work

The ways in which Two-Spirit men see themselves as unwanted by their communities can overwhelm how they see themselves as Native peoples. At the same time, Two-Spirit organizations such as the Green Country Society and the Denver Society focus on giving Two-Spirit men the opportunity to "be Two-Spirit." Being a Two-Spirit man, as I was often reminded, goes beyond simply being Indian men who have sex with other men, which is how most non-gay Indians see them. Rather, it is a way for people to be part of a historic gender-diversity tradition, which is how the men see themselves. In order to do this, Two-Spirit men are actively negotiating tribal and popular Native American culture, as well as sexuality and gender difference, to create cultural practices that are distinctly Two-Spirit. These cultural practices are a syncretism of strict traditional tribal ceremonial practices, popular supra-Indian identity, and contemporary gay identity. This syncretism proves to be a way for Two-Spirit men not to completely turn away from their Native, or tribal, identities, but rather as a way to resist the kinds of oppression discussed in the previous chapter.

Meeting Two-Spirit Needs with Ceremonialism

In all my discussions with Andy, from the very first, he emphasized unremittingly the need for Two-Spirit people to be involved in spiritual activities. Andy was by far the most vehement about the necessity for Two-Spirit people to connect with either their individual tribal spirituality or participate in a Two-Spirit ceremonial community. Andy's efforts were focused on providing opportunities for Two-Spirit people to learn and be involved in ceremonial practices. The logic of Andy's approach is that a spiritually committed Two-Spirit person was more likely to find his/her way to self-acceptance. Also, Two-Spirit persons who had specialized knowledge, such as how to conduct ceremonies, would be less likely to be judged solely on their sexual orientation and would be more likely to find their way back into a significant role in their tribal community.

As a result of Andy's push for spiritual solidarity, the Denver Society placed a particular emphasis on being a ceremonial community through their perfection of ritual knowledge and practices. In fact, many Two-Spirit societies across North America consider the Denver group to be the religious specialists of the larger Two-Spirit community. Often they would be invited to other Two-Spirit societies' gatherings to "bring the spiritual component" by holding sweat lodge and pipe ceremonies and advising Two-Spirit people on the ways they could bring more spirituality into their social practices. One of the essential functions of the Colorado society is teaching Two-Spirit people Native spiritual ways through weekly meetings and their annual Wenakuo gathering. Andy describes the purpose of providing this service for Two-Spirit people:

We needed to begin the work. Start a school, if we can use that analogy. We needed to actually begin teaching people how to go back to this spiritual role. Realize that we had to go back to the basics for most people, such as learning what the medicines are, how to interact with an elder in how you treat them, how to show respect. We had to teach stuff that many people learn and take for granted in our community. A lot of people hadn't been around their tribes; some had been adopted and raised by whites. Some of them had parents who rejected Indian ways.

To help this situation, I went to some Two-Spirit elders and told them that I wanted to start a camp for teaching, and I asked for their blessing. And they told me that they would support such a camp.

Andy himself was one of the people who had "lost contact" with the spiritual part of being Indian as a young man removed from his tribal community. In an attempt to "do the work" of teaching people to fulfill their traditional roles, Andy began to expand his own knowledge of ceremonial practices. Prior to organizing the Wenakuo gathering with the input of Sheila and Glen, Andy had been studying under some Lakota elders.

— Andy: *At this point I had already been assisting a woman who would put people on the hill [vision quest] and other ceremonies. I had been working side by side with her and she was teaching me all the ceremonies. She was giving me the work to do, and I was also helping my uncle Will. I had already gone on the hill, but I knew giving this knowledge to other people was something we had to do.*

Andy shared his knowledge with other people in the Denver group and also relied on group members who had extensive experience with their own tribal ceremonial practices. Eventually, with the knowledge that Andy had gained from willing elders and the help of other Two-Spirit people, in 1998 the Denver group held its first Wenakuo gathering north of Colorado Springs. At the first camp they "put someone on the hill" for a vision quest and held pipe ceremonies and daily sweat lodges. Two-Spirit gatherings sponsored by other societies included activities such as pipe ceremonies and sweat lodges, but they also included drag shows and other nonspiritual components. Consistently, I was reminded that Wenakuo was only for ceremony and ceremonial training.

— Andy: *We learned that this was something very much needed in the Two-Spirit community. It was very different than the other gatherings because it wasn't a place just to come together and laugh; it was a place of prayer. Everything we did was teaching people how to not be destructive, but to be prayerful.*

Over the years we have had the camp, and many more people come each year. What this told us is that we were doing things right. It was a space where people were able to come together as a community, cohesively, and learn the things they needed to learn so they could again walk the spiritual path and take on those roles in their own communities.

The ceremonial culture of the Denver Society is decidedly Plains-focused and relies heavily on the Seven Rites of the Lakota. Andy explained that the Lakota focus is influenced by three factors. First, Denver was a major relocation city for Lakota people in the 1950s and continues to be a place where there is a significant accumulation of older, spiritually knowledgeable people and younger people (including gay men) escaping reservations. Second, and more importantly, Lakota elders and medicine people were the only Natives in the Denver area willing to help Two-Spirit people find a spiritual focus. Third, the Lakota people are one of the few societies that have a historical memory into the 20th century of multiple gender roles. Therefore, some of the people Andy worked with had knowledge (mostly through legend) of the actual roles that gender-different people took in that tribal tradition and could provide vital information on the "right way" to incorporate their role into ceremonialism. Andy also assumed that a tribal culture that most recently had an intact place for the gender different would be the most likely to accept Two-Spirits becoming involved.[1]

My first experience with the Denver Society's spiritualism came early in my research, at the 1999 Wenakuo camp. There I attended a sweat lodge conducted in the Lakota way. Shortly after the ceremony began, I noticed that many of the men and women participants did not know the songs or prayers of the Lakota lodge, me included. To keep the ceremony going, Andy passed a hand drum and asked specific people to sing spiritual songs from their own tribal cultures. People who knew the songs sang along, attempted to sing along, or sat reverently quiet. There were no fewer than 15 tribes represented in that sweat lodge, and of that number, more than half sang spiritual songs from their own ceremonial cultures. I was impressed by the way Andy had used the form of the Lakota sweat lodge as a foundation for a ceremony that came to include such a diverse group of people. The lodge was conducted much like any other Lakota sweat lodge in that the ceremonial details were intact, such as the way the heated rocks had been gathered, the order of entry into the lodge, the number of times the lodge door was opened, and the sequence of events inside the lodge. Yet Andy had effectively included tribal differences, such as having a female fire keeper and smoking a "women's chanupa" (pipe) after the lodge, without disturbing, as he explained it, the fundamental values and content of the ceremony.

Andy's efforts at making ceremonial practices accessible to everyone was not without controversy. Some Two-Spirit men, particularly those of Lakota and Dakota ancestry, criticized the ceremonial practices for being incorrect and some of the participants and leaders for their lack of knowledge. They felt that Andy's attempts to include everyone had greatly diluted the content of the ceremony and had the potential of "doing harm." Some people pointed to the Winds Dance held at the Wenakuo as an example. I did not witness the Winds Dance, as I arrived the day after it had been held, and Andy politely refused to discuss it in detail with me. According to some of the other Two-Spirit men present at the dance, it was based on fundamental components of the Sun Dance. There was a center pole and other poles representing the four directions. Dancers fasted the day before the ceremony, and a flesh offering was taken. The singers performed Sun Dance songs, as well as ceremonial songs from other tribes. One of the dissenters commented: "This dance is made up. It is supposed to be some sort of Sun Dance, but people were singing powwow songs. No one here even has permission to be doing something like this. Andy has just overstepped his authority. I know he means well, but we have to consider that we are not ready for this kind of thing as a community, and we can't go around making up stuff."

Disagreements over the ways Andy attempted to make Lakota spiritualism the "standard" Two-Spirit spiritualism do not overshadow the ways he brilliantly adapted spiritual practices to Two-Spirit ideas about gender and sexuality. The greatest impact of Andy's vision of Two-Spirit ceremonialism was the emphasis it placed on incorporating the various gender and sexuality differences that Two-Spirit men and women brought to Native society. Two-Spirit gender ideology is founded on the fundamental idea that gender is fluid, and people can move in and out of degrees of femininity and masculinity as a particular situation demands.[2] Women and men therefore should be allowed to seek social and spiritual roles within a community based on their felt gender rather than the sexual dimorphic equivalent to their genitalia. In the way he taught, spoke about, and practiced spirituality, Andy adapted Lakota and broader mainstream Native spiritualism, with its specific gender roles for men and women, to Two-Spirit people's gender and sexuality.

In practice, Two-Spirit gender logic proposes that women at the drum are not really women, but are women who have a manly spirit. With Andy's efforts, men who feel that they are more womanly, or women who are more manly, have the opportunity to realize that feeling within a Native ceremonial context. That is, the women who desire to be a singer at a drum, which in many tribal societies and powwow culture is seen as a male-only pursuit, are given the opportunity to learn songs and sing within a ceremonial context. Women are also given the opportunity to undergo the training to lead sweat lodges, go on male-style humblechayas (vision quests), and dress in men's regalia. Men are also free to take on female dress and roles such as providing blessings, singing women's songs, and cooking ceremonial meals. Within the context of Two-Spirit ceremonies and gatherings, men and women are allowed to transcend the kinds of gender regulation and bias against their sexuality that had previously made them reluctant to participate in tribal society. Andy also emphasized that the Wenakuo and other Denver Society spiritual practices give Two-Spirit men and women an opportunity "to heal the forced separation between one's gender, sexuality, and indigenous identity." The opportunity to act out and live one's felt gender is important, but it is also important for Two-Spirit people to gain spiritual enlightenment from the ceremonial practices.

Ceremonial gender bending not only reorients Native cultural practices toward Two-Spirit ideals but also provides an opening for Two-Spirit participation. Because Two-Spirit ceremonialism is adapted to include gender and tribal differences, Two-Spirit men feel less self-conscious about their participation in tribal and mainstream cultural practices. Andy stated with pride, "Two-Spirit people are getting to practice ceremonial roles in ways that they couldn't among their own communities." The benefit, according to Andy and others, is that Two-Spirit people are being allowed to heal from the pain of alienation, homophobia, and self-hatred. Ben added, "They also are building self-confidence that will allow them to stand up to their families and communities and to no longer be ashamed."

Men "Shaking Shells"

The inspiration of Andy's ceremonial gender bending was also realized in the ways the Oklahoma group members challenged the gendering of the Stomp Dance. The Stomp Dance is a ceremonial dance practiced by the peoples originally from the southeastern United States such as the Cherokees, Creeks, and Seminoles. These societies brought the Stomp Dance ceremonies with them to Oklahoma upon removal, and the dances have become a point of solidarity.[3] Stomp dances in Oklahoma take place in the late evening at remote locales known as grounds. Gender roles at most grounds are strictly defined. Men lead the ceremonial songs and women "shake shells."[4] "Shells" refers to the rattles of turtle shells or evaporated milk cans filled with river rock that women wear around their calves. During the ceremony, a line of dancers snakes around a ceremonial fire following a male song leader who calls out the words to the songs. The women shake their rattles by stomping behind the men. At most stomp grounds, dancers fall into the line alternating between male and female. When dancing at their family's grounds, Two-Spirit men adhere to the structured nature of gender roles. Most men assume that taking on the female role of shaking shells at the stomp grounds would be met with considerable disapproval. However, at Two-Spirit stomp dances the men are offered an opportunity to change their ceremonial roles.

The only formally organized Two-Spirit stomp dancing, "stomp" for short, takes place at the GCS annual gathering. Each night of the gathering everyone slowly gathers in the courtyard outside the dining hall for after-dinner stomp. After saying a short prayer, the first song leader, usually Sean, begins by striding around the fire and calling everyone to the dance with a loud "Ohhhh" and the sound of shaking shells. Most of the leading falls to Sean because he is a frequent leader at his ancestral stomp ground. Sean may mix gender roles at the gathering by shaking shells at the same time that he leads songs. In addition, he may mix the gendered symbols of the Stomp Dance by wearing a skirt, shells, and a hat with an eagle or crane feather attached at the top, which is a common symbol worn by a man to indicate he is song leader. As Sean begins to circle the fire, other Two-Spirit men fall in behind him in no specific gender-role order, calling out the words of the songs. Many of the men wear shells and stomp skirts, while others readily adhere to the male roles during the dance.

For some of the men, Two-Spirit stomp dances are the first and only place that they stomp dance. Despite being of Southeastern descent and having families involved in "grounds life," some of the men never felt welcome to participate in their ground's dances. Zach, a Two-Spirit Creek, told me that when he was a child and teenager he preferred the work and ceremonial roles of his female relatives. As he grew older, he felt continual pressure to perform male-defined roles such as learning to lead songs. By the time he was to be initiated into grounds life as an adolescent, he had lost interest in participating with his family in stomp dances. As a young adult, he had stopped going to the grounds altogether and had not been to a ceremony in ten years. Like many Two-Spirit men, Zach felt that his family and his stomp ground's community did not accept his gender identity or sexual orientation and that there was no place for him there. Before heading into the circle to shake shells, Zach said, "I can dance here at the gathering how the Creator intended me to . . . as a Two-Spirit person." When I asked why it was important for him and other Two-Spirit men to be able to wear shells, Sean confidently stated that he sees his Two-Spiritedness as giving a special meaning to shaking shells. Sean feels that by mixing gender roles he is "bringing together" the spiritual separation between male and female in the Stomp Dance. He stated, "Two-Spirits shaking shells helps create a balance between the female and male energies at the ceremony. It is how it used to be at the grounds a long time ago."

Ironically the multitribal environment of the Two-Spirit Stomp Dance had brought Zach, Jason, Sean, and other men closer to their Seminole, Creek, and Cherokee cultural heritage. Participation in anything tribally specific was a distant childhood experience for most. Yet the freedom to dance created a noticeable change in the ways some of the men viewed themselves and their ancestral communities. Jason, for example, told me, "When I stomp, whether they are Creek or Cherokee songs, I feel more Cherokee." Jason went on to explain that he felt connected to a past that was "taken from me personally" because of how his family viewed his sexual orientation and his desire to be gender different. Participating in the Stomp Dance also seemed to reconcile the men's feelings of invisibility within Native society and the inaccessibility of tribal cultural practices. Learning and perfecting the songs of the Stomp Dance made Sean noticeably more confident and outgoing.

Over the three years that I had regular contact with Sean, I noticed, as did others, the considerable effort he put into learning songs, shaking shells, and making contacts among Stomp Dance people. Sean's efforts made him somewhat of a cultural authority admired by other Two-Spirit men. People admired Sean for his knowledge but also his eagerness to get other men involved in Stomp Dance. As is traditional among some Stomp Dance cultures, the leader gives a speech right before or after the opening song. On multiple occasions, Sean took this opportunity to encourage men of all ancestry, but particularly those of Southeastern decent, to learn the ways of their people. He detailed the ways Stomp Dance had helped him heal, and brought him closer to his family. Stomp Dance had helped bridge the gap between him and his family in a way that he had not known since before he recognized his sexual orientation. In one oratory, Sean emphasized Two-Spirit people's need to accept "who we are" and be active in "finding our place within tribes" through being socially and spiritually involved. For Sean, the path to self-acceptance was one that led back to tribal society through "forcing communities to realize their loss by not accepting Two-Spirit people."

While Sean and others seek to be accepted by their communities as Two-Spirit people, they also relish their time away from dominant Indian and tribal culture, because it allows them to be who they are in ways that would confuse most non-gay Native peoples. That is, they can be gay and Indian at the same time.

Indian Camp

Two-Spirit men spend a considerable amount of time thinking about and working toward involving themselves in Native social and spiritual practices as a way to resolve their alienation. In a similar way, with their own style of communication, humor, and conversation topics, Two-Spirit men resist the regulations on their behavior imposed by non-gay Indian social contexts. This resistance is found in the ways the men creatively bring together popular gay and Indian cultural influences. Despite the men's tendency to view the gay community as hostile, they do not completely turn away from popular gay culture as an influence in their lives. Remembering that most Two-Spirit men's first experiences as gay men were in their local gay community, it is no surprise that many of the men have incorporated those influences into their attitudes and behavior. At the same time, Two-Spirit men cannot help but modify these cultural influences to meet their own need, which is to make gay culture Indian. We further see their syncretistic approach to being gay and Indian in the creation of what Sheila and I came to call "Indian camp." "Camp" or "campiness" is a common concept in popular gay culture. Camp often refers to a form of expression that flamboyantly exaggerates feminine verbal and nonverbal behaviors. Camp takes on many forms such as exaggerated hand movements, tilting of the hips when making a point, and the use of such terms as "sister" or "girl" in reference to another male (Michasiw 1994). However, as Cameron and Kulick (2003) and Harvey (1998, 2000) point out, camp talk is not simply substituting feminine terms for masculine ones. Rather the focus should be on "how particular kinds of juxtapositions in language are used creatively to actively construct particular identities and social positions" (Cameron and Kulick 2003:102). "Indian camp" can best be described as Indian teasing and humor combined with the flamboyance of popular gay attitudes. It is also where the dominant discourse of Indian male hypermasculinity is juxtaposed with the gender conceptions of Two-Spirit men. It is through this juxtaposition that Two-Spirit men tease loose definitions of what it means to be Indian from dominant ideology and make them available for use in alternative ways. Indian camp not only provides a compromise between the seemingly different discourses of mainstream Indian and gay cultures, but also negotiates Two-Spirit differences with mainstream notions of gay behavior.

The essence of Indian camp resides in the creative ways Two-Spirit men generate their own linguistic cues, style of humor, and topics of discussion. Gay male themes, such as sexual conquest, are manipulated by adding Native terminology and cultural context. For example, men refer to having a sexual encounter with another man as snagging. The word "snagging" is used widely among Native peoples to denote an intimate encounter with another person, but it is a foreign term among the gay community. Therefore, the phrase snagging would be unintelligible to non-Indian gays, but the idea of referring to snagging as something that occurs between two men is unintelligible to non-gay Indians. The Two-Spirit use of the term to describe their own intimate encounters bridges this cultural divide. Two-Spirit men's expressions of Indian camp relied on these nuanced juxtapositions of gay sexuality and culture with Native cultural influences. This interplay of gay and Indian involved the creation of an attitude that was distinctly Two-Spirit.

Those people who were new to the social world of Indian camp seemed lost when faced with laughing cues, punch lines, and teasing. The first time I attempted to insert a quip into the milieu, all laughing ceased and I received only blank stares in addition to a look of shameful disapproval from Sheila. It was clear that I had learned how to interpret the humor of Indian camp, but was not anywhere near (or welcome to have) proficiency. The humor and teasing style most resembled that of your average Indian community. Indian humor can vary from tribe to tribe, but contemporary mainstream Indian humor parlays social and economic struggles into the material of jokes and teasing. It has been noted by numerous scholars that Native people use joking as a way to deal with some of the hopeless aspects of their situation. Also, they use teasing as a way to create community solidarity and as subtle cues to control inappropriate behavior. As Keith Basso (1979:67) points out, joking is a way to soften stiff interpersonal relationships over time.

Two-Spirit men use the community-building aspect of Native humor style in their own unique way through adding references to femininity, teasing other men, and telling stories of sexual conquest.

I finally picked up the nuances of Two-Spirit teasing the moment when Sean parlayed one of my unsuccessful joking attempts into teasing Sheila about her hairstyle. I told Sheila, after she had been living in Oklahoma for six months, that she was in danger of becoming a "perm res," as in "permanent resident of Oklahoma." Sean saved my lame joke by saying "Aaayyeee, but she sure does have a rez perm," as in "reservation permanent" (hairstyle). The humor of the "rez perm" lies in its reference to stereotypes about how people adapt on "the rez" (reservation), such as using bailing wire for a door handle to a house or driving a car that only has one gear. Therefore any perm that one would get on a reservation would surely be done at home and lack the up-to-date style one would find in a salon. This expression of teasing would not be out of place in any Indian social context, particularly among women. However, what made the joke Two-Spirit was the fact that Sean crossed a gender barrier to tease Sheila about a topic from a woman's domain. Furthermore, the joke was shared not among women, but it involved a gay man using a feminine-oriented joke to tease a man living as a woman. The use of a feminine joke in male contexts would no doubt be used to challenge another man's masculinity. In this way, however, Sean had adapted the genre of teasing to fit within the more open gender rules surrounding conversation and potential topics that Two-Spirit men share.

Another memorable moment of teasing came while we were singing a closing song after a GCS weekly meeting. Earlier, before the meeting began, Robert was telling a story about a guy that he had snagged with the weekend before. As the meeting progressed, people took every opportunity to make jokes about Robert's promiscuity, inserting comments about "needing to keep his skirt down and his legs closed" and "cruising at the park." The teasing came to a finale during a song containing the phrase "hey ya ho." Every time the men sang the word "ho" (popular slang for "whore"), they pointed to Robert. This pointing at Robert in synch with the word "ho" continued through their attempts to sing the song correctly despite being in the throes of laughter. Playing off the word "ho" in the powwow song, the men were making fun of Robert's promiscuity.

Crucial to Indian camp are the ubiquitous references to femininity and the use of feminine forms of address. Two-Spirit men often referred to one another as "sister" or "girl." One of Ben's favorite expressions was to call everyone "chica" or use the drawn-out word "girrrlllll-ennnne" when replying to a shocking statement. Two-Spirit men incorporated these forms of address into quips such as "Sister, I wanna have his babies" when seeing an attractive man. Sheila, when asked by someone going out if she needed "anything from the store," would make a reference to being "out of tampons" or say "bring me back a fireman." The Denver group, or the "Denver Divas" as they came to be known, had developed several funny and linguistically contagious feminized forms of address. They became most known for the falsetto-pitched exclamation "Ahhhwww," with an emphasis on the "Ahhh." The "Ahhhwww" was mostly used in response to a teasing remark and was an integral part of group teasing where the men would try and outdo one another's quips. Usually the quips involved teasing someone for being promiscuous, "trashy," or "bitchy." On most occasions these teasing sessions involved four or five people sitting around telling stories. One such session involved Sheila telling a sexual conquest story.

The sexual conquest story embodies all the crucial elements of Indian camp, such as references to femininity and a healthy dose of parody. Sheila was always willing to provide a detailed and humorous story about a sexual conquest. Sheila had so many sexual conquest stories that many men speculated on their factuality. Yet no one challenged Sheila because it would be rude to call someone a liar, but more importantly, her storytelling was so good, and the incidents often outlandish, that it was always a pleasure to listen.

Sheila always had a willing audience for her stories, and one particular night at Willey's was no different. It was Sheila's first time back in Denver in four months. People were buying her drinks and it seemed that every Indian in the whole bar was coming over to talk to her. This guy came over and started talking to us. He was particularly interested in Sheila, especially after she told him she was part Hopi. After they talked about where they were from, Sheila started describing a sexual conquest with the fancy dancer the Hopi guy was talking about. She was telling the story about hooking up with the guy in the camper on his truck while she had her jingle dress on. The Hopi guy spread his arms in the air like they were legs and said, "I bet those jingles were just going 'swish, swish, swish'" while moving his body back and forth. A chorus of ahhhwwws spread throughout the group, followed by intense laughter. Sheila replied, "Oh yeah, later I had his two friends. I rode up on my pony [making the movements of daintily riding a horse and shyly drawing a bow and arrow], captured them, and just took them back to my tipi," followed by a chorus of ahhhwwws and laughter. And Paul immediately replied, "Yeah, she let them go back to their wives in the morning. I don't think they were going to be the same, girl," followed by another set of ahhhwwws.

In addition to the more campish "Ahhhwww," Two-Spirit men also make use of the "lulu," which is a common form of exclamation used by Native women. The "lulu" is a high-pitched trill where the tongue is fluttered against the roof of the mouth. Among Native North Americans this is a sound only made by women. Women "lulu" during the singing of songs or when showing support to someone, and it is fairly common within mainstream Native culture. For example, if someone is being honored at a powwow, the women in the audience might lulu as a sign of agreement with the honor. Women who are singing backup at a drum will place lulus in specific parts of the chorus to add emotion. Two-Spirit men make use of the lulu in similar ways. The men would often use the lulu as a way to show support for a statement made by someone or as a greeting. On the opening day of the GCS gathering, one always knows that a chorus of lulus signals the recent arrival of attendees. In this context the lulu is used as a greeting, but also, as Sheila said, "Because it's men luluing, it lets them know that they are in a safe place, where things are different."

The continuous bouts of ahhhwwws, teasing, lulus, and outrageous storytelling seemed to have a transformative effect on any space Two-

Spirit men occupied. Indian camp provided an attitude and a way of interacting that was distinctly Two-Spirit, a "lavender lexicon" that found its way into any space where Two-Spirit men were.[5] Non-Indian gays and non-gay Indians might recognize some of the fundamental forms of Indian camp, such as cultural irony (Sheila's riding the horse and drawing a bow), but the combination of Indian cultural irony and gay sexual irony is largely intelligible only to other Two-Spirit people. In this way it becomes a vehicle to challenge their alienation but also provides a grounding from which Two-Spirit men can innovate.

Miss Indian Hills Princess

In the same way that Two-Spirit men transformed camp by adding Native cultural context, they also worked their syncretistic magic in combining the competition drag show with Indian princess titles. The Miss Indian Hills competition is a longstanding tradition at the GCS annual gathering and has developed into an all-out drag show competition for the title of princess. On Friday night after the evening meal, the sandstone National Park Service meeting hall at the campground is transformed into a stage and audience area. A karaoke machine is brought in; someone is appointed DJ and put in charge of coordinating music with the performers. Performances themselves involve no reference to Native regalia or traditions, except for the occasional intertribal humor. Participants make a point not to "kitschify" traditions of female Native symbols in the drag show. As one person pointed out, "As tempting as it is, it would be disrespectful to do a Pocahontas routine because it would involve using regalia." Rather, participants' parodies of women follow typical drag show performances. However, unlike popular gay drag shows that emphasize the perfection of parody, the Two-Spirit "no-talent show" relies both on the quality of the act and on the courage it takes to perform. The routines use pop music by "divas" such as Barbara Streisand, Diana Ross, and Celine Dion. The emcee introduces each performer by a stage name, usually a feminized form of a name, such as Christique for Chris.

Popular gay society has city or regional titles for professional female impersonators. Gay bars and social or political organizations will often sponsor a drag competition or pageant and include their name in the title, such as the "Miss Denver AIDS Coalition."[6] These competitions follow the format of beauty pageants, award prize money, and require the winner to appear at other gay community events for one year. Individuals are judged based on their ability to parody women, their talents, and their commitment to the social and political causes of GLBT people. Among female impersonators, these titles hold a significant amount of respect and are highly competitive.

Drag and other titles are not totally unlike powwow or Native organization princess titles. Native social groups, such as Indian veteran societies, as well as tribes and individual powwow committees, will sponsor princess competitions. States such as Oklahoma even have a "Miss Indian Oklahoma" pageant. The young woman who is chosen to carry a princess title must represent the organization at other powwows and pageants. The women who win these titles are chosen in the same ways as beauty pageant contestants; they are selected for their commitment to tribal and Native social and cultural values. The girls who carry princess titles are held in high regard in their communities and are usually given a place of honor during powwows and other events. The winner of the Miss Indian Hills competition is given the same level of respect among the Two-Sprit community and is expected to represent the GCS at other Two-Spirit events and within the larger gay community.

Most of the performers in the Miss Indian Hills competition only "do drag" once a year at the gathering and have no professional performance experience. Some people begin practicing their routines and assembling their outfits months before the gathering. Others are more spontaneous and decide to perform hours before the contest. A few performers do drag professionally in gay bars, but most do not. Nonprofessional performers see the gathering as the only "safe place to do drag." Because popular gay culture is predominantly white-oriented, Indian men are reluctant to draw attention to themselves through drag performance. Gathering performers see the talent show as an opportunity not to be judged according to their race, class, and social position, as they assume they would be within popular gay contexts. Instead, performers assume that their acts will be judged according to a gay Native standard.

The role of emcee at the Miss Indian Hills competition combines the glamour of a drag show announcer with the subtle Indian humor of a powwow emcee. Just as powwow princesses are held in high regard, so too are the colorful and clever emcees who keep powwows lively and moving in an orderly fashion. Older and experienced Indian men are favored as emcees at powwows, in the same way that the gay community draws on established drag queens to announce during drag show competitions. In both of these communities, announcers can earn a reputation for being funny and knowledgeable. Being a good and well-liked powwow emcee or drag show announcer carries considerable cultural capital, and can provide additional income in the form of tips for the drag announcer and an honoring for the powwow emcee.[7] The emcee of the Miss Indian Hills competition acts as a conduit to bring these two traditions together for gathering participants.

For as many years as the gathering has been held, Jolene, whose off-stage name is Joe, has emceed the Miss Indian Hills competition. Jolene emerges from the back kitchen door to face vibrant pop music and bright lights in the large dining hall–turned–stage. Jolene, a six-foot-three Apache drag queen, who is a well-known drag show announcer in the gay community, always begins the show with one of her own acts. One of her favorite opening songs is "I Will Survive." Besides doing performances herself, Jolene's job is to ensure that the individual acts get properly introduced, that the audience remains entertained, and that protocol is followed in judging. Jolene's job is also to bridge cultural worlds by introducing the performance of "the lovely Visa DeCarte" and making a joke about "How do you get Indians to line up for a photo? . . . You say cheese." Jolene's regular gig is announcing at her local gay bar, where Native people are rarely found. However, at the Two-Spirit drag show, Jolene combines the campish feminine references to drag, such as "I can't believe she can do that in heels," with the tribal jabbing and Indian humor one expects to find at powwows.

As the performers are announced and come on to the stage, the people in the audience clap along to the music, give dollar bills to the performers, and raise encouraging applause. Performers are usually dressed in sequined gowns, heels, wigs, and heavy makeup. While lip-syncing to the words of the music, they walk and dance around the stage using the mannerisms of female pop singers. The acts differ in how well each person "pulls off" their parody of women. Some of the men look painfully uncomfortable dancing and singing in women's shoes and dresses. Yet moving elegantly and naturally in women's clothing is the sign of a talented drag queen, such as Jolene or Christique, who have both won the competition.

During the show each of the contestants must perform two songs. After the final contestant's performance, Jolene tallies the judges' scores backstage while the performers change their outfits for the announcement of the winner. While the audience waits, the reigning princess says a few words about what the past year as princess meant to him. Alex gave a particularly moving speech at the 2004 gathering. He told of how he was "scared of his own shadow," but the honor of being Miss Indian Hills had inspired him to be more active in the Two-Spirit community, which had helped him be more comfortable with his sexuality.

After the break, all the contestants line up and Jolene announces the third- and second-place winners, who are given flowers. The winner is given a sash that says "Miss Indian Hills 2002" in the style of powwow princesses. In addition, the winner receives a crown, which sometimes is a tall and elaborate beaded crown, similar to the ones worn by female powwow dancers. During the convocation the exiting princess will place the crown and sash on the new princess. The princess will wear her crown and sash during the grand entry at the gathering powwow on the following night. The rules of the competition also dictate that Miss Indian Hills will make the sash and crown to be given at the next year's retreat. Although not all Miss Indian Hills princesses have done so, they are expected to represent the GCS at the annual Eagleton gay pride parade as well as other Two-Spirit events across the country.

It makes perfect sense that Two-Spirit men combine the two worlds of gay community (the drag show) and Native cultural performance (the Indian princess). I was frequently reminded by the things Two-

Spirit men did and said that they are products of two cultural realms and that these two cultural realms were largely mutually exclusive until the creation of Two-Spirit communities. Two-Spirit men may involve themselves in their tribal communities as well as the gay community, but neither social realm appears to contain all that Two-Spirit men need. The cultural innovation of Miss Indian Hills challenges the forced divide and sets the stage for other amalgamations of Indian identity and difference.

Queering the Powwow

Two-Spirit men readily employ gay community influences when doing drag or teasing one another, but they are as serious about their participation in Two-Spirit powwows as they are about their ceremonies. Just as mainstream Native society uses the powwow as a means of emphasizing "Indianness," the Two-Spirit powwow emphasizes both Indianness and the sex/gender diversity of "Two-Spiritedness." By dressing in regalia, dancing, and simply being present, the men at the Two-Spirit powwow reaffirm the traditional nature of their identity. In this way, Two-Spirit powwows allow individuals to incorporate their sexuality and gender identity into Native social practices, as well as to access the cultural practices that generate traditional Native identity. As Two-Spirit powwows are private affairs not advertised to the general public, the men feel free to express their gender identity and sexual orientation in a Native cultural context.

The powwow as a form of traditional cultural participation fits nicely into the structure of the Two-Spirit men's community based in what Sanchez (2001:51) calls "intertribal negotiation." While Two-Spirit men may not come from the same tribal ceremonial traditions, most have been to powwows and are aware of regalia categories and powwow etiquette. Powwows do not require large amounts of specialized knowledge; therefore, Two-Spirit men with various levels of involvement in traditionalism can participate. This is important for many of the Two-Spirit men who may have little experience with the traditions of their specific tribe but can relate to their "nativeness" through the powwow. Also, because powwows are not tied to the specific practices of one particular tribal tradition, they are easily modified to reflect regional influence and social agendas such as sobriety, and can be varied in size. In a similar way, the flexibility of the powwow as a cultural form allows Two-Spirit men to modify the focus to reflect their specific needs, such as making an explicit connection between their ideas about sex and gender, and Indian cultural identity in public Native social contexts.

From the beginning of my time with the GCS, Ben had been talking about his desire to dance in female regalia at the gathering powwow. I was fortunate enough to witness his dream coming to fruition. The first time Ben entered the gathering powwow arena in his female Southern Cloth regalia, he beamed with satisfaction. Everyone seemed impressed with the ease in which he stepped and his shawl swayed to the grand entry song. Along with the recently crowned Miss Indian Hills, Ben and other Two-Spirit men, dressed in both female and male regalia, followed the flag and eagle staff into the dining hall powwow arena. The drum made up of Two-Spirit men and friends or family pounded out the grand entry song with the volume of a major contest powwow. Of the men who wear female regalia at the gathering powwow, a few live as women full-time, and for them this moment is not a switch. However, for the other men who dress in female regalia, the gathering is an opportunity to express an aspect of their identity assumed to be unacceptable in Native social contexts or with their families. Ben had spent the last year not only perusing pawnshops around Oklahoma looking for a Southern Cloth dress, moccasins, and the other necessary items for female regalia but also seeking advice from female dancers on how to properly assemble his regalia. Ben assembled a woman's yellow trade cloth dress, purchased matching moccasins, had a few things made, and adapted a beaded belt from his male regalia. Knowing the significance of this moment for Ben, a few people gave Ben shawls to match his regalia at the gathering giveaway.

At powwows around Oklahoma, Ben is usually a male straight dancer, but at this gathering he was fulfilling a long-held desire to powwow dance in female regalia. For Ben, this "switch" represented reconciliation with years of struggling to adapt his sexuality and gender identity with his Native identity. Ben often pointed out that his family suppressed his desire to dress feminine or participate in female-oriented activities such as playing with dolls, sewing, cooking, and joining in with women at social events. Ben saw his participation as a woman in the gathering powwow as a way to take back the years of shame he had endured because of his gender identity, and honor "the child who knew what gender it wanted to be." The switch also brought with it a change in Ben's usual role at the gathering powwow. By dressing in female regalia, Ben had to change his role within the powwow from previous years. For instance, he no longer carried the eagle staff into the arena during grand entry, a role usually reserved for men. Ben's switch also affected the way I related to him during the powwow. After having gourd danced with Ben for years, it was a difficult adjustment for me to have him dancing behind me as a woman, instead of beside me as a male dancer. However, Ben easily fell into women's powwow roles and seemed to be quite comfortable in his new regalia.

Two-Spirit men do not view gender mixing, or switching, in contexts defined as Native, as a form of drag. Rather, redefining traditional gender roles in gathering contexts is informed by the symbolic content of traditional expressions of gender within Native culture. Therefore, Ben adheres to the standards set by the dominant Indian community for proper female regalia and behavior in the powwow arena. At the same time, Ben does not completely forfeit certain male-defined roles. Even though he now wears female regalia, he continues to freely address powwow participants without speaking through someone else, as women are often expected to do at mainstream powwows when they want to make an announcement or honor someone. As Ben told me, gender at the gathering is not as much about switching from one gender to another as it is about feeling free to express one's degree of maleness or femaleness outside the confines of contemporary Native gender ideals. Two-Spirit men see their choice of regalia as a reflection of their gender as well as something fluid that can be modified according to context. A few Two-Spirit men will switch to female roles or female dress at different times during gatherings, while many will mix gender components in dress and "women's work," such as preparing meals and cleaning up afterward.

The men's practice of mixing gender roles at the powwow closely mirrors the situational conception of gender they employ. That is, most Two-Spirit men (except those that desire to live as women full-time) do not desire to completely switch to female roles. Rather, as I was reminded, the men are keeping with historical ideas of gender, where the gender different drew on multiple sources of gender identity in any one context. Accordingly, Ben wearing women's regalia, but also taking on the male role of "speaking for people" during the powwow, signals a mixing rather than a complete transformation. The role that one takes at the powwow is seen as a reflection of the degree to which they feel more male than female or vice versa. This expression of gender is also context dependent, in that someone may prefer to be more male at the powwow while being more feminine in their choice of activities such as sewing or cooking.

Like most powwows around Oklahoma, the gathering powwow has a grand entry, round dancing, giveaways, emcee, and specials. However, the gathering powwow is different in the ways traditional gender roles are modified while adhering to traditional powwow activities. It is not uncommon for Two-Spirit men to do the "Indian two-step," a couple's dance usually with a partner of the opposite sex. During the dance the man and woman stand beside each other and hold hands out in a crossing manner in front of themselves. Usually the head lady and head man dancers lead the two-step, guiding dancers around the drum, moving randomly about the arena, and having people switch partners in a way similar to square dancing. At mainstream powwows, married people, dating couples, and people "eyeing each other" will be the ones to two-step. Occasionally adolescent girls will dance together, but one would never see two men two-stepping together, even in jest. Two-stepping at powwows, holding hands, and the occasional peck are privileges the heterosexual majority enjoy in Native social contexts. The Two-Spirit powwow not only gives the men opportunities to hold hands or dance without fear, but more importantly allows them to associate their sexuality with Native social practices in ways not usually available.

Being able to express one's gender identity through the powwow is important for Two-Spirit men because it is a culturally sanctioned reflection of their Native identity. Powwows are used to introduce people "entering the circle," for teaching traditional values, and as a tangible source of Native identity (Mattern 1996). Accordingly, participation in powwow dancing is a recognizable source of Native identity for most people, Native and non-Native. By holding a powwow at the gathering, Two-Spirit men are using this multitribal practice in the same way as other Native peoples. However, Two-Spirit men are using powwow tradition as a forum in which to express something particular to their situation as gay Native and gender-different men. Through Ben's wearing of female regalia, the powwow as a cultural practice is transformed from a mainstream-Native-sanctioned source of identity to one that emphasizes Two-Spirit interpretations of Indianness, both public and felt. In this way, the gathering powwow, like any larger powwow, becomes a space in which traditional Native identity is reinforced and made.

Ben dancing in Southern Cloth also creates a public space for representations of Two-Spirit identity. Because the traditional public positions of Two-Spirit men are absent from most contemporary Native ceremonies and practices, Two-Spirit men lack a public forum in which to express their identity. However, the gathering powwow seeks to resolve the lack of such opportunities. At the gathering, Two-Spirit men can be not only publicly Indian but also publicly Two-Spirit. Ben characterizes his switch as carrying the same symbolic power as other forms of public expressions of Indian identity. Two-Spirit men are being publicly Indian in their regalia and redefining the meanings associated with traditional practices. Forecasting a time when his gender switch will be acceptable, Ben said, "Someday through our persistence we [Two-Spirit people] will make it OK for me to go into the arena in my female regalia, and I won't have to fear other people's reactions."

Better Women

Two-Spirit men's attempts to bridge the divide between their gender proclivities and their Native identity did not occur only at Two-Spirit community events. Rather, it was something that they engaged through their choice of hobbies and interests. Almost every conversation I had with Sheila included a discussion of beading, crafts, or techniques of regalia making. Sheila is well known in the Two-Spirit community as the quintessential Indian craftsperson. Her beadwork is truly astonishing and is coveted among Indians, Two-Spirit and not. Sheila is continually making new dresses, beading buckskin outfits, making medallions for extra cash, and sewing regalia for other people. Almost every Two-Spirit person I know who participates in Indian events that require a certain kind of clothing, fan, staff, rattle, or drum makes that item himself. It seemed that every time I saw Ben, Sheila, Carl, Jeff, Sean, or Glen, they had made a new piece of regalia, added to their regalia, or were working on a project for someone else. The degrees of ability and style vary, but on the whole, people continue to perfect their abilities in crafts and regalia making. In fact, several people criticized my own beadwork for "not getting any better" and me for not trying to come up with more intricate and difficult patterns. The perfection of one's regalia is common in Indian Country, especially when people are competing in powwows. However, Two-Spirit people see crafting as part of their historic role, and to some extent they see sharing their abilities with others a responsibility. A lot of people would echo my assertion that the best beadwork I have ever seen has been done by Two-Spirit people.

Historically, gender-different people were often recognized as what Lang refers to as "better women" due to their talents in sewing, potting, weaving, cooking, caring for children, and other kinds of women's work (1998:241). Early anthropologists noticed among the Winnebago, Hopi, Lakota, Mohave, Zuni, and Crow tribes that the gender different were well known for their handicrafts as well as their hard work keeping their families provided for (Lang 1998:201, 241–246). Because historic

Two-Spirit people did not have the burden of child care responsibilities or menstruation, their gender ambiguity allowed them to focus on perfecting handiwork and also permitted them a flexibility in the kinds of cultural activities in which they participated (Lang 1998:241–257; Roscoe 1991:166–169; Williams 1986:58–59,). Whitehead (1993:109) and Williams (1986:59) have theorized that historic excellence at women's work was an attempt by "berdaches" to find a substitute for the prestige that could be obtained in masculine domains such as war and hunting. That is, berdaches were to have transferred their "standard male socialization emphasiz[ing] competition for prestige" to the work of women (Williams 1986:60). For Whitehead, berdaches seeking prestige was a device to reinforce biological male dominance through filching women's modes of production, thereby reinforcing structural inequality against women (1993:109). However, Lang sees excellence in women's work more about individual gender ambivalence, not a substitute for masculine prestige, and more representative of the kinds of activities available to particular individuals (1998:244–246). She states: "They demonstrated masculine prestige-seeking behavior in the masculine role components they retained, and they exhibited feminine prestige-seeking behavior in the feminine role components they practiced" (1998:245).

Within the debate over the historical importance of excelling in women's work, I tend to agree more with Lang's interpretation that seeking prestige is more of a common cultural value that crosscuts gender lines and modes of production. However, within this book, being a better woman in contemporary Indian society could be conceptualized in yet another way. As I have argued, concepts of Two-Spirit identity are steeped in the cultural performances that are required of one to be considered legitimately Indian. I would argue that being a better woman in contemporary Two-Spirit society is also based in meeting the discursive requirements set out by the Indian community. Therefore, contemporary excellence in the performance of women's work has as its goal a connection with historic roles, as well as the goal of perfecting the kinds of activities and symbolic content valued for Indian *people*. By perfecting beading, jewelry making, camp cooking, regalia making, and performing female ceremonial and powwow roles, Two-Spirit people are meeting the discursive requirements set out by the Indian community, while articulating with a specific set of gendered activities.

As many Two-Spirit people have detailed in their stories, an affinity with the female members of their family and activities associated with feminine characteristics were very important at a young age and were seen as promoting their perfection of women's work. Historically, gender-different people served to keep the elder women company while learning to perfect tribal material traditions (Williams 1986:59). In similar ways, contemporary Two-Spirit people draw a connection between their social involvement with older women and their proclivity for women's work.

— Ben: *I was always around my grandmother and learning how to cook and sew. When I was three years old there is a picture of me with a dress and a shawl on. My mother told me that I was so comfortable in wearing a dress and that role. If I got to be around grandma and those female things all the time, then I probably would have been ok. But my parents made me feel ashamed for liking women's things.*

Ben's feelings were echoed in many of the stories I heard Two-Spirit people tell. Most showed an interest in arts, crafts, cooking, and sewing at an early age but were discouraged from such activities because they did not meet the cultural expectations of their biological sex. Several people recited how their parents openly discouraged their participation in female-related activities through ridicule or physical means. Despite parental efforts at discouraging feminine cultural behaviors, most of the Two-Spirit people I knew could at least sew and cook well.

Sheila was particularly influenced by contact with the elder women of her family. Sheila often detailed to me stories about how she began beading and sewing at an early age with her grandmother. One afternoon Sheila and I were at her sister's house outside Denver, and she began pulling beadwork items out of a large black garbage sack. She began showing me beaded medallions, moccasins, vests, armbands, necklaces, and just about any item on which one could sew a bead. As she pulled the pieces out of the bag, it occurred to me, as she explained how each item came to be, that the pieces represented a stage in Sheila's personal development as a Two-Spirit person. She explained that she would often go to her grandmother's house and sew with her. She learned the intricate details of Plains-style beading, regalia making, and sewing Indian-style clothing from her grandmother. Many items in the bag were ones for which she had received her grandmother's instruction. During the time Sheila was learning from her grandmother, she was not living as a woman, and was dancing male fancy and traditional powwow styles. She showed me the boys' regalia she had made herself, and as we moved chronologically to her early teens she began showing me the women's regalia she had begun to wear and dance in. It was in the powwow dance performances that Sheila began to locate her transformation from publicly male to publicly female, but it was also in the making of regalia, where she attempted to perfect traditional knowledges.

Sheila characterized her attempts at perfecting traditional crafts and public performances as becoming a better woman. Sheila's ability to bead, dance, and cook better than other Indian women is a point of pride for her and often recognized by other people. She made the best fry bread, managed to bring meals together with little food for large numbers of people at gatherings, and would give consultations to other people on the crafting of regalia. After she moved to Oklahoma she was approached by many people to make regalia items and beaded princess crowns. In one instance Jeff was making a pair of moccasins to trade for an eagle bustle. However, the man with the bustle, after seeing Sheila's fully beaded buckskin, wanted Sheila to make the moccasins instead of Jeff. Sheila, as well as other people, saw the demand for her work as an affirmation of her Two-Spiritedness as well as her "better woman" status.

The ways in which people were recognized as better women or worked within female-influenced traditions in some ways articulated with stereotypes about gay men as the best hairdressers, decorators, dressers, cooks, and listeners. Matt is recognized as being a "flawless hairdresser," and many of the GCS group members would have him do their hair before retreats and powwows. Sean not only beaded but also made beautiful stained glass pieces, painted, and is recognized as a talented interior decorator. Ben is recognized for his abilities as a cook, spiritual person, and an intent listener. Each person seemed to have a specialty that he brought to the group, and in doing so, made his talents available to other people. Therefore, at meetings, gatherings, and retreats, various people were called upon to be in charge of making meals, saying prayers, emceeing the drag show and powwow, teaching crafts, and organizing.

One example of making talents available to others was the six-month collective effort to assemble Robert's straight dance regalia. Sheila was responsible for the sewing involved in making the broadcloth leggings and trailer. Jeff and Carl assembled and beaded a dance stick and eagle fan. Glen helped with making the beaded bandoliers, and Ben provided the eagle feather worn on the top of the roach. Because Robert did not have contact with many people in his family, and they did not participate in Indian society, the other Two-Spirit people pooled their efforts so he could be ready for his powwow debut. These people fulfilled tasks that would have been done by the female members of Robert's family. That is, most straight dancers' mothers, sisters, or grandmothers tailor their ribbon shirt, leggings, breechcloth, and trailers. They are also usually responsible for beading the dance stick, constructing the fan, and making moccasins. As we watched Robert dance in the arena in his new regalia, someone said, "Now everybody will want Two-Spirits to make their outfits."

The recognition of themselves as working toward the perfection of Indian material traditions goes far to legitimize Two-Spirit access to Indian social worlds. As we see with the demand for Sheila's handiwork, Indian people recognize quality and distinctive craft traditions. However, most important about the perfection of Native material traditions is its obvious and distinct connection with the Indian community. That is, many Two-Spirit people excel in designing, crafting, and performing according to community standards of the ideal. They adhere to the unspoken rules surrounding beading styles, dress patterns, and ritual performance.

Self- and Social Acceptance through Cultural Compromise

The conception of Two-Spirit as a different kind of person, separate from mainstream gay society and connected with traditional Indian culture rooted in the historical record and cultural memory, challenges dominant Indian ideology about gender difference. It also requires Two-Spirit men to actively make connections between their sexuality and gender identity and contemporary Native/tribal cultural practices. Because contemporary Native practices are seen as having historical roots, Two-Spirit men must also reify the connection between historical gender diversity and their contemporary expressions of that identity. To people outside Native societies, a man "shaking shells" may lack controversy, yet Indian people in general are resistant to alterations in the cherished contemporary traditions that also happen to simultaneously endorse a heteronormative version of Native identity.

Throughout this book I propose that Two-Spirit men's effort at combating the heteronormative assumptions that alienate them involves a cultural compromise between Native culture and gay desires. As we have seen, the creative modifications that Two-Spirit men engage in, such as the Two-Spirit powwow, do not have as their goal to completely alter the fundamental values behind Native traditional social practices. Rather, they are altering rules, such as gender regulations about who can or cannot perform ceremonies and who has the right to be legitimately considered a jingle dancer. In so doing, Two-Spirit men are making room for their needs but maintaining the intelligibility of the tradition.

The ultimate goal of making gender diversity and alternative sexualities intelligible aspects of Native traditions, and thus identity, is to locate a space for "Two-Spirit" within dominant assumptions about what is rightly considered "Indian." The path to social acceptance resides in that association. As Two-Spirit men will tell you, accepted forms of Indian identity are inherent in the social practices that reinforce community solidarity and individual identity. This, then, is why Two-Spirit men seek the acceptance of their families, tribal communities, and Native people in general, knowing as they do that the majority do not accept Two-Spirit men's sexuality and lifestyle. For their entire lives they have heard about the ways Native peoples have resisted cultural domination from outside, and they themselves have seen the ways their communities have struggled to successfully incorporate change into their cultural practices. They have also seen the ways that their community members use their Native identity and community support to negotiate their way through life. Within these struggles they have seen that Native people are willing to change, adapt, and more importantly recover traditional knowledges and practices.

CHAPTER SIX

Mending the Hoop

Two-Spirit men's efforts at cultural compromise go largely unnoticed by their tribal communities. Two-Spirit men also feel that they have an obligation to their individual tribes and Indian people in general. While Two-Spirit sexuality and gender identity is structurally denied expression in mainstream Native society, the men are actively attempting to make a place for themselves within contemporary Indian communities by being useful. The goal of this engagement is to "mend the hoop." The hoop the men are referring to is the medicine wheel. Two-Spirit men feel the hoop was damaged when Indian societies began to no longer incorporate sexuality and gender difference into their cultural practices and identities. For Native North Americans the medicine wheel represents the cycle of Indian life in space and time. Health advocacy movements such as alcoholism treatment use the concept of completing the hoop as a metaphor for individuals coping with their alcoholism. That is, a portion of the circle is missing or damaged because an individual's medicine is not balanced as the result of internal strife caused by substance abuse.[1] The only way for individuals to be at peace with themselves and their disease is to complete the hoop through recovery and thus return to balance. Two-Spirit men feel that the hoop representing Native society is thrown out of balance by homophobia and their estrangement. The hoop is also a metaphor of hope for a time when the medicine wheel will be completed by the acceptance of Two-Spirit men and women. Mending the hoop becomes a metaphor for a time in the future when, as Ben pointed out, "Two-Spirit men can participate in their communities without fear and can be helpful to Indian people."

Being Useful

Two-Spirit men realize that non-gay Indians will not serendipitously one day understand and accept sexuality and gender diversity. Rather, they see the process of mending the hoop as one of empowering themselves. Part of this empowerment comes from creating roles for themselves within their tribal communities and Native society. The men conceptualize creating roles for themselves in terms of being useful. Two-Spirit men feel they must make themselves useful to communities through taking care of the needs of the people. Therefore, once they are recognized as valuable members of Native societies, non-gay Indians will see the value in accepting them, and attitudes will change. To reach this goal Two-Spirit men critically engage Indian community values in their attempts to address social issues they perceive are not fully dealt with by Indian peoples.

Statements in previous sections explained that Two-Spirit men place the blame for the decline in acceptance of sexuality and gender diversity on the lack of public roles and incorporation for them in Indian society. Two-Spirit men also clearly connect their lack of public roles to the social problems of Native communities. Many people feel that without Two-Spirit men there to create balance, Indian society will continue to suffer. Ron echoed this when he told me one night in an intense conversation, "The spirit of the people has been broken by white ways. This is why we don't have Two-Spirit people anymore. This is why Indian people have so many problems. You understand that life is a hoop, and our people are a hoop. We need to repair that hoop." Two-Spirit men see part of Indian society's ills or the lack of completeness in the medicine wheel as a result of the intolerance for difference. Sheila, Glen, Andy, and Ben all felt that Indian society's domestic problems and the problems of the youth were related to a lack of stability between masculine and feminine energies in Native communities. A conversation with Glen demonstrates this idea:

— Brian: *Some of the people I spoke with tell me that the reason that Indian people have problems is because they have lost a sense of diversity in their communities and purpose for all kinds of peoples. Would you agree with them?*

— Glen: *Yeah, I would agree with them. That reminds me of the guy I was telling you about that runs the Sun Dance. He told me, "In the old times we never had child abuse, we never had spousal abuse, because we had the Two-Spirit men there to stand between the men and the women." One of the roles of the Two-Spirit men was to protect the women and the children from the men. We know how men can be aggressive. In the old days just the presence of a Two-Spirit person in camp would calm the men down. Now that there aren't Two-Spirit men in our communities like the old days, we have child abuse, spousal abuse, and so much divorce. One of the big reasons for that is there are no Two-Spirit men in the communities to stand between the men and the women because we know what it is to be both.*

The theme of the medicine wheel is repeated through the ways that Two-Spirit men's presence and activities are felt to create a societal balance. By representing a combination of male and female traits, Two-Spirit men seek to balance the forces that men and women bring to a society.

As with Two-Spirit cultural performances, they conceptualize their social roles as flexible according to the specific needs of the community. Two-Spirit men see themselves as balancing not only the energies between men and women but also the various "things that need to be done" in Indian communities. They see their ability to transcend the gendered aspects of the social, spiritual, and political as allowing them a freedom of movement between various roles that communities need filled.

— Ben: *If we can become people who can help ease the load on some of our medicine people, politicians, chiefs, old ladies, then more power to us. It's what you do to benefit the society.*

As I was frequently reminded, "It is not enough just to show up." Rather, Two-Spirit men assume Indian people are not going to welcome them without their having a function in communities. Therefore, Two-Spirit men perceive that they must prove themselves to non-gay Indians as a way to negate the complications created by their sexual and gender identity.

— Glen: *We have to prove to the community who we are. If people come out first they may never get a chance to prove who they are. People may cut them off and not let them be a ceremonial leader. When people find out you're gay, you already have so many strikes against you. If you come to*

*people and they know you are gay, plus you are ignorant of your culture,
then it will be twice as hard. We have to prove ourselves, that we give something good to the community.*

—Ben: *We have got to get over the hurdles they present about us being gay.
It is almost like we need to do twice as much as everyone else, just out of
respect until we can get our foot in the door. I'll do whatever it takes except
jeopardize who I am.*

*We have to start getting back involved with the Indian community. If we
are fortunate enough to have families and people to help us get back into
the community, we need to start by just being seen. Once they see that we
are honest about our feelings, then they will open themselves up to us holding a larger part in ceremony and powwow and society. Sharing a part of it
is the first step to healing that Two-Spirited hoop.*

— Sean: *Once the people see what we can do, then they will be like, "We
don't really approve of it, but we will let you dance." Then they'll be like,
"They know what they are doing so it is ok." Eventually it will be, "We are
glad you're here to dance" and maybe it will someday be "Won't you come
please dance with us?"*

In an attempt to fulfill their commitment to communities and
thereby mend the hoop, Two-Spirit men actively engage social issues
within the Indian community. Although people such as Andy emphasize the ceremonial role of Two-Spirit men, they have made more significant progress toward community acceptance through their commitment to social causes. Two-Spirit men have dealt with the absence
of traditional public social roles by becoming active in areas where
communities lack resources, interest, or knowledge. They are combining traditional Indian values with contemporary necessities to fulfill
the needs of their tribes and Native peoples in general. Taking up causes
for HIV programs and working with youth are not tasks assigned by
Indian communities. Instead, they represent areas where Two-Spirit
men have an interest and over time have developed their participation
and knowledge to a level that Native peoples have come to depend on.
Two-Spirit men would conceptualize this subtle assertion of their pres-

ence in communities as a form of resistance having the potential to alter attitudes toward their differences. As Sheila's sister pointed out, "They have to figure out what works for them. It may not be the traditional ceremonial route, but maybe more of a combination between the traditional and the contemporary. This is a way they can achieve being Two-Spirit and utilizing their medicine by helping to educate the greater Native community."

Caring for Children

Two-Spirit men further conceptualize their mending of the hoop by taking on the caregiver role and teacher for children in their families and in their communities. Historically, Two-Spirit men were known for caring for children in their kin groups and taking on parental roles for orphaned children in the tribal communities (Williams 1986:54–55). Contemporary Two-Spirit men also feel a necessity to care for children in their family, as well as to teach children about Indian cultural ways. As is prevalent in many Indian communities, children are often cared for by multiple family members. Many people I know had taken on the role of aunt and uncle for children within and outside their families. When they were called upon to help with the raising of a female child, they emphasized their ability to teach young girls female cultural ways. They were called upon as well to help with male children. For example, Andy and Mike both were taking a major role in the raising of their sisters' fatherless children.

— Andy: *We come from a matriarchal family, where women make all the decisions. Most men who have married in can't handle that and end up leaving the family. We end up having to raise the children, which is fine because we get to raise them properly.*

In line with his statement, Andy has taken on a caregiver and teacher role with his sister's children. Since he has both a niece and a nephew, Andy is required to instruct them on both male and female cultural expectations. He taught the niece to sew, make regalia, cook traditional Southwestern foods, perform female ceremonial tasks, and helped assemble her dance outfit. Also, he taught the nephew the ceremonial and social requirements of being a Puebloan man. His niece and nephew frequently accompanied him to ceremonies and gatherings where they would be given tasks such as gathering firewood and cooking. Andy characterized this role as one requiring a Two-Spirit person because their mixed gender roles made them more knowledgeable of both male and female cultural expectations. Also, because a Two-Spirit person was teaching them, young people were learning a respect for the diversity in Native society to which they might otherwise not have been exposed.

Mike helping his niece through her rite of passage presents an exceptional example of a Two-Spirit person being called upon to fulfill a traditional role. Mike's sister has a teenage daughter, Theresa, whose father left when she was very young. Mike took on the role of providing money, clothes, and support for the little girl. Since Theresa had no aunts, Mike's family called upon him to prepare her for "becoming a woman." As Mike explained it, his people's tradition requires a young girl approaching puberty to go through training where she learns to pot, weave, cook, conduct domestic ceremonies, and accomplish many other activities required of an adult woman. He told me it was expected that he take on the teacher role with his niece since he was the Two-Spirit person in the family. Mike said that traditionally, a Two-Spirit person would teach young girls how to be women, since they had the time and knowledge to nurture female children. Mike spent a year teaching Theresa how to silversmith, weave, butcher meat, keep house, put on makeup, and make her hair into a traditional style, as well as various other female-oriented tasks. Mike's family had not always been accepting of his sexual orientation, and it was not until recent years that they began to accept him. He felt that his teaching Theresa the "right ways" helped demonstrate his knowledge of his tribal culture but also proved that he was bringing particular gifts to the community.

The children that Two-Spirit men cared for and taught were not always in the men's own families. Jeff's role in maintaining an Indian youth organization is another example of the ways Two-Spirit men are asserting themselves through meeting community needs. Jeff lived in a small rural community where he worked with an Indian youth organization primarily made up of teenagers. Part of his job was to counsel at-risk youth, as well as organize cultural activities with an Indian focus. Jeff went well beyond the requirements of his job to the extent of giving up weekends and evenings in support of the youth. A considerable number of Indian families in the area are among the working poor. As with many Indian communities, alcoholism and child neglect are major issues, as well as adolescent criminal activity, teenage pregnancy, and substance abuse among youth. Part of Jeff's task was to use cultural programs to help the teens work through their specific issues while teaching them about Indian culture. Jeff told me that he saw his commitment to this work as fulfilling his required role as a Two-Spirit person. He saw himself as ideal for the job because he had the nurturing aspects and cultural knowledge of women and the stern aspects and cultural knowledge of men. Jeff was often also called upon for help when youth group members needed emotional support. He looked at his work as meeting needs not being met by the youth's parents, families, or the tribal community. Jeff put a considerable amount of time into teaching the youth Native cultural ways, such as instructing the girls on how to bead and assemble their dance regalia. He was also teaching a group of young men to powwow sing so that they could start performing at events. Despite seeing his work as fulfilling the roles of a Two-Spirit person, he remained in the closet in his community and with the youth. I heard that one of the active older people stated that he knew Jeff was gay but did not care because Jeff had "gotten a lot of kids off drugs and taught them about their culture."

Some Oklahoma members took on teaching and mentor roles with gay youth in particular. One of Ben's adopted sisters had a son who had recently come out. Ben was asked to talk to and help his teenage nephew deal with coming-out issues, as well as instruct him on the role of Two-Spirit men. Mick had a nephew who had recently come out, and his family asked him to teach the child to be a good Two-Spirit person. Ben and Mick both told me that they were glad to do the work of helping these teenagers avoid the problems they had encountered when they came out. For instance, Ben went to great lengths to ensure his adopted nephew's exposure to the healthy gay lifestyle promoted in the

Two-Spirit organization and society. He was continually emphasizing to the young man that his indigenous identity separated him from mainstream gay society. Ben's nephew went with us on numerous outings to powwows and ceremonial dances. Ben was also working with him to assemble his dance regalia. As he reiterated, "Part of our job as older Two-Spirit men is to make sure that our young Two-Spirits don't get abused by the gay scene."

Doing HIV/AIDS Work

Issues of HIV/AIDS were largely ignored in the Native community early in the epidemic. Indian communities saw the disease as something associated with white gays and urban drug users, hence its designation as the "white man's disease." As Roscoe has pointed out, the HIV/AIDS epidemic did not begin to be addressed among Indian gays and lesbians until the late 1980s (1998:103). At that time, the concern over HIV/AIDS was primarily focused in the urban gay and lesbian Indian communities and had made little headway into the rural and reservation-based communities. From the beginning of the epidemic through 1988, the Centers for Disease Control (CDC) did not have a separate category for Native Americans with HIV/AIDS, which exacerbated the effects of an already underreported number of infected Indian people. However, by 1990 the CDC established the National Native American AIDS Prevention Center and urban activist groups had begun addressing the needs of Native peoples with HIV (Roscoe 1998:105).

It is recognized that gay and lesbian Natives themselves had much to do with the establishment of Native-specific HIV programming in the United States. Since the late 1980s, several organizations designed to support HIV-infected Natives have been established. Ahalaya in Oklahoma City, the Navajo AIDS Network, and the San Francisco Native American AIDS Project are just a few of the "model" organizations that seek to provide counseling and testing services, meals, housing referrals, and some medical treatment for people infected with HIV/AIDS. In the early 1990s many of the aid organizations turned to issues of prevention, seeking to educate Indian people on the virus and issues surrounding it. Individual tribes and Indian nonprofit groups began receiving funding for HIV/AIDS prevention, which led to the establishment of many Two-Spirit groups such as the GCS. More recently, the focus on HIV/AIDS has turned from a gay Indian focus to one including all Indian people, particularly youth.

In the effort to educate Native people about HIV/AIDS, Two-Spirit men have found an additional way to serve communities. Almost every Two-Spirit person I interacted with had done some kind of AIDS work. AIDS work was similar to that conducted by the non-Native gay community, which included caring for individuals infected with the disease, visiting and providing food for incapacitated individuals, providing rides to the doctor, giving donations, and volunteering for outreach and fundraising events.

Early in the epidemic Andy and Mick began working to create awareness among the mainstream gay communities, and eventually turned their efforts toward indigenous gays and lesbians.

— Andy: *Back in the early eighties when I began looking at how we were going to get the prevention message out to the gay community, I realized that there wasn't really a community, because the only thing they have in common is attraction to the same sex. What I realized was that in the indigenous community, we already have a community. Then the question became how we move within the indigenous community to create change.*

Through my conversations with Andy and Mick it became obvious that making indigenous people aware of the risks and issues involved with HIV/AIDS is incredibly more difficult than doing outreach among the gay community. The first obstacle is addressing the issue of sexuality in public Indian contexts, particularly same-sex relations. Mick detailed to me numerous occasions of encountering hostility toward gays, lesbians, and individuals infected with the disease during his presentations. Mick found that many of his initial contacts with tribal health organizations focused on the morality of the issue or its association with same-sex relations. Nonetheless, Mick and Andy made it clear that by the early 1990s, HIV/AIDS was taking a toll in both gay and non-gay indigenous communities and it was their role to address it through public action.

Ben, Mick, Phillip, Andy, and Roberto all were employed in positions that required HIV/AIDS outreach to indigenous communities with mostly a rural or reservation focus. The clinic that employed Ben and Mick required that they run the GCS, do public outreach at powwows and other events, and travel to conduct training and information sessions at tribal headquarters. Mike worked for a local interfaith Christian organization that provided public outreach and counseling for Native and non-Native individuals who were at risk for or had contracted HIV. Andy mostly worked within the Two-Spirit community writing grants and organizing retreats and other Indian activities to help in the prevention education effort. Roberto worked for his tribal health agency and did public outreach on and off the reservation. The public outreach work usually required some level of self-disclosure, and all the people I knew who did this kind of work were openly gay and often forthcoming about related issues.

Mick is one of the first people to have done public outreach with tribal health workers and communities in reservation and rural areas. He had numerous anecdotes about the homophobia and misunderstanding that he encountered on these initial visits. Most of his seminars were daylong workshops given for tribal health workers and youth counselors and included basic information on HIV/AIDS, how it is contracted, and who is at the highest risk of infection. Inevitably, community recognition that the gay men in their communities were at the highest risk raised a certain amount of controversy. No one disputed that gay men were at the highest risk, but rather they argued that there were no gay men in their communities. Any outreach event that Mick conducted included some form of discussion of the history of sexuality and gender diversity among historic Native American communities. Predictably, any discussion that Mick presented conflicted with popular opinion among attendees. Despite resistance, Mick has persisted in his outreach and awareness activities. In many ways, programs such as those sponsored by the Red Cross or CDC owe considerable gratitude to early Indian HIV/AIDS activists for opening the door to education while risking their own alienation from their communities. Now that issues surrounding HIV/AIDS are starting to become "de-gayed," the presentation of workshops is less controversial.[2] Mick's early efforts no doubt made considerable strides in the acceptability of discussions of sexuality and disease in Indian communities. In fact, presentations and training on HIV/AIDS at tribal headquarters occur frequently with little incident and are required for anyone working in health and youth areas.

As Roscoe points out, "The fight against HIV/AIDS is of necessity a fight against homophobia" (1998:107). In similar ways, Two-Spirit efforts at making Indian communities aware of HIV/AIDS issues brings sexuality and gender diversity into the public discourse. Through their efforts at creating awareness about HIV/AIDS, they are also speaking out on behalf of differences in the Native community. All the people I know who did HIV/AIDS-related outreach included gender diversity in some component of their presentation. They were using the public space provided by communities as a way to not only create awareness of their presence but also show their concern with Indian peoples. Roberto's effort at HIV/AIDS outreach within his own reservation community is often recognized as one of the most dangerous situations. Working in his own community puts Roberto at a certain disadvantage that other people working in HIV/AIDS may not encounter, in that he is making himself more vulnerable to community biases and homophobia, which could result in alienation or violence. When we were all sitting around discussing this issue, Roberto felt that it was his duty as a member of the tribe and as a Two-Spirit person to make the community aware of the risks. He also felt it was important to reach out to the Two-Spirit men in the community and "let them know they aren't alone." As in Roberto's efforts, most HIV/AIDS work among Indian people involves some aspect of outreach to Two-Spirit men. The goal is not only to help them remain healthy but also to relieve a sense of isolation surrounding their identity. Roberto, as well as many other people, felt that isolation on reservations and rural areas led Two-Spirit men to live secret sex lives in cities and other places. Many also felt that this secrecy and isolation was a major factor in HIV/AIDS infection among Indian gays and lesbians. Roberto brought HIV/AIDS and sexuality issues to the people in his workshop through stories and by using traditional methods for the teaching of knowledge. Using the components of oral tradition, he would tell stories about the importance of individuality, respecting one another, and respecting oneself, as well as sing songs about Two-Spirit men and staying healthy.

Two-Spirit men were the first to address issues of HIV/AIDS in Native communities, and much of the burden of the early work fell on their volunteerism. By asserting themselves through public outreach efforts, Two-Spirit men have become the experts in the area of HIV/AIDS work. It is often assumed that an individual who goes to a tribe or other Indian organization to present a workshop or training on HIV/AIDS will be a Two-Spirit person. One non-Two-Spirit person I know who works with HIV/AIDS in Indian communities is often assumed to be a lesbian. Ben was quick to point out that Two-Spirit men made the best counselors for issues of sexuality since they could relate to both genders and multiple sexual orientations. Now many tribal governments who are expected to provide some kind of HIV/AIDS training for their workers and awareness for their youth are turning to the people who are recognized to have the required knowledge for the work. As a result, there are more openly gay individuals working as counselors in Indian hospitals and clinics and in nonprofit organizations catering to Native communities.

The clinic where the Oklahoma group is based always has a booth among the craft and food booths at major powwows in the area. Ben and Mick spend a considerable amount of time sitting in the booth during the events, handing out brochures on safe sex, and distributing condoms from a small basket on a table. The selling of crafts and food is a major aspect of powwows, and people spend a considerable amount of time browsing sales booths during events. A clinic booth handing out condoms would previously have been a considerable disjuncture within the world of Indian crafts and fry-bread stands. However, young people are often the ones who stop and pick up condoms and brochures. The distribution of condoms does occasionally bother some people, but as Ben said, "That doesn't keep us from going through two four-hundred-count boxes per powwow." At one particular powwow, I noticed a youth organization had begun handing out "snag bags" – paper bags containing condoms and a brochure with information on sexually transmitted diseases and birth control. When Ben and I walked past the booth, he commented that "we were the first to do that," but he was glad other people had taken up the effort, as well as catering to the youth through the play on "snagging." Accordingly, it is often recognized by Two-Spirit men and non-gay Natives that the early work on HIV/AIDS by Indian gays and lesbians (and their families) helped make awareness efforts such as handing out condoms at powwows acceptable.

In order to understand how recognized differences can be used strategically as a vehicle for resistance, I have illustrated the ways Two-Spirit men use social and discursive opportunities in an attempt to make their identity intelligible. Exploiting "openings" in the social structure provides an opportunity for Two-Spirit men to make performances of their identity part of the public discourse. For example, Two-Spirit men use their knowledge about HIV/AIDS prevention to fulfill a need in the community. By fulfilling the need, they are making their identity part of social relationships and thereby making Two-Spiritedness a recognized social identity. In arguing that Two-Spirit men resist social alienation by exploiting dominant ideology, I have attempted to show how "Two-Spirit" has the potential to be recognized as an aspect of "Indian." In examining the ways Two-Spirit men exploit dominant ideology, I also demonstrate that discursive forms of resistance compliment other forms of resistance to challenge alienation and structural inequality. In the concluding chapter, I draw heavily on the idea that structural inequality frames the dialectic between power and difference, as well as between representation and social belonging.

CHAPTER SEVEN

Difference and Social Belonging
in Indian Country

As the members of the Green Country and Denver societies would agree, Two-Spirit people do not represent an alternative form of Indianness. Rather, they are and see themselves as committed to formally accepted community standards of social behavior and moral responsibility. Nonetheless, Two-Spirit people represent a contradiction with dominant perceptions of a masculinity that is inherited from historical constructions of Indian men. Two-Spirit people, however, perceive Indian societies' endorsement of the masculinist standard as a contradiction of the traditional values that emphasize the social acceptance of all differences. As we have seen, Two-Spirit identity is in part an attempt to reconcile inherited and traditional attitudes toward difference within communities. Notions about difference are enfolded into the ways all Indian people distinguish themselves from white society as well as make distinctions between each other in tribal traditions, religious beliefs, blood quantum, politics, economics, social class, and sexual orientation. In this way, Two-Spirit identity is representative of the ongoing struggle between multiple forms of difference.

In an effort to reincorporate their uniqueness into contemporary Native communities, Two-Spirit people strategically emphasize their cultural sameness with Native communities while deemphasizing sexual orientation as a personal defining characteristic. In doing so, they make use of community-recognized historic and contemporary tribal and supratribal Indian traditions. The use of these traditions acts to ensure a recognized connection with the Native communities in which they grew up or seek participation. The incorporation of dominant Native ideology into notions of what Two-Spirit represents creates a reliance on specific traits recognized as "Indian" within multitribal notions of race, gender, and cultural practice. Despite their "perfection" of Indianness, Two-Spirit people assume that any indication of their sexual orientation will not go unnoticed, and as a result any gendered or sexual transgression will generate hostility from their respective communities. Two-Spirit people perceive that acceptance in Native communities hinges not only on the fulfillment of ideal Indianness but also on how communities perceive their sexual orientation. In this way sexual orientation as a socially recognized difference becomes the single greatest alienating factor for Two-Spirit people in perception and reality. As we have seen, members of the Oklahoma and Colorado groups employ several strategies in dealing with alienation, which include (1) remaining in the closet, (2) changing rules governing performance out of dominant community view, (3) outright public displays of performative resistance, and (4) making oneself useful in Native communities through HIV/AIDS activism and caring for children. While these strategies have differing results, and are somewhat contested among Two-Spirit people, they represent ways of finding a place in communities. While finding a place in a community is crucial to what it means to be Two-Spirit, it is also an example of the ways identity is actively constructed at the intersection of difference and social belonging.

Notions about individual and group difference in the construction of identity can be seen in the various ways Two-Spirit people interact with each other and Native communities. Difference as a personal attribute is manipulated as a way to emphasize sameness with the larger Native community, while it is also used to signal individual uniqueness. Individuals may at one time define themselves as simply Indian, while drawing on representations of distinct tribal traditions. By using individual differences as both an incorporating and exclusionary device, non-gay Indians and Two-Spirit peoples unwittingly invoke power relationships. That is, differences take on social meaning and are given the power to include and exclude individuals based on a constant comparison to ideal types of "Indianness," "Creekness" (as a tribal example), or "Two-Spiritedness." As we have seen, ideal types of Indianness range from dominant masculinist standards to Two-Spirit perfection of women's work, and from tribal membership to social participation. Whether we are speaking of the dominant Indian community or the GCS and Denver Society, representations of difference – racial classification, masculinity and femininity, individual and collective behaviors – come to determine individual understandings of social belonging.

As Two-Spirit men effectively construct ideas about their Native, gender, and sexual identities in relation to dominant ideological standards, they also critically engage the several crucial contradictions in Indian cultural identities. For example, many Indian communities perceive a loss of cultural practice and values among their people, while they are preventing and regulating the participation of individuals eager to commit themselves. This contradiction remains the most frustrating for Two-Spirit people who spend a considerable amount of time perfecting Native practices and living according to Native values. Accordingly, many people who identify as Two-Spirit realize that they are not wholly prevented from social participation, yet they perceive that participation is dependent on adhering to dominant expectations of male-bodied persons. As a result, Two-Spirit people's identity embodies not only dominant expectations but also the contradiction with community standards that it represents. They may perform an expected role but their personhood still differs from dominant ideology. As Glen pointed out after winning second place in men's straight dance competition, "If they knew I was a queen, they'd take away that honor." In this way we can understand Two-Spirit frustrations of continually riding the edge of acceptance and alienation. Also, we can come to see that acceptance and alienation become a set of experiences that depend upon individual difference.

Epidemics of Difference

On a run into town to get more flour for fry bread, Zach, a Two-Spirit Apache I was not very well acquainted with, told me a story about the ways his community has reacted to his HIV status.[1] Zach began by telling me that he had been in a coma and almost died several years before when his T-cell count hit a devastating low. While in the coma he was hospitalized in a reservation Indian Health Service facility near his community. Zach's family held ceremonies in his room throughout the ordeal. As Zach tells it, the ceremonies resulted in his eventual recovery and return home. He had spent several months resting at his parents' house and came into very little contact with other people on the reservation. It was not until someone refused to shake his hand at a wedding that Zach realized that the nurses at the hospital had broken confidentiality and revealed his status to others in the community. Out of fear that it would upset him and cause a decline in his health, the family did not tell Zach that they had experienced ridicule from other people in the community. They also did not want Zach to know that many nurses and other workers would not care for him and that during his stay in the hospital, Zach's family had to bathe him and change the sheets. By the time Zach discovered the talk surrounding his "status," most people in the community had already heard. I asked Zach how he felt about his HIV status changing his status in the community. Holding back tears, he responded that he was very angry at the people in the hospital for telling everyone and not caring for him, but he was mostly disappointed in "his people." He pointed out that whenever someone is seriously ill in his community, his people, even professional health workers in the hospital, come to the spiritual and physical aid of the ill person and his or her family. Zach said that he knew of only two community members not related to him that attended ceremonies or cooked meals and took care of children for his family while they were attending to him in the hospital. For Zach, the community's attitude about his illness was contrary to traditional values of helping out community members. Also, Zach perceives that the social stigma he and his family suffered due to his illness is the result of a breakdown in traditional values, which in his words makes his community "no different than white people."

Homophobia and the stigma of HIV/AIDS challenge community notions of care. In many cases, once individuals are infected they return to their reservation communities to seek help and rely on the notion that they will spend their last days with their families. However, I heard of multiple occasions when individuals returned only to be ostracized by their families. Although some families take care of their HIV-infected family members, there is a considerable amount of shame in the form of public social stigma. Fearing public shame leads many individuals to isolate themselves to the family home and limit their community participation. When communities become aware of a person's declining health, family members refer to HIV as "cancer" or say that "the doctors aren't sure what it is." As Ben and other HIV/AIDS workers pointed out, disguising illness may save individuals and families from experiencing additional grief, but it further perpetuates social stigma as well as the silence about HIV's effects on Indian people.

Also, as Zach's story illustrates, seeking care in tribal hospitals poses a further problem related to community perceptions of HIV/AIDS. Patient confidentiality is a significant problem at tribally run hospitals. Fears about their HIV status being revealed and resulting social stigmas make it even more unlikely that infected individuals will seek care in tribally run facilities. Outside traditional healing, for many infected Natives, tribally run facilities are their only health care option. Therefore, few opportunities exist for infected people to get treated without coming into contact with community members. Because tribally run clinics and hospitals lack adequate funds, physicians and administrators are often placed in the position of having to choose between outrageously expensive HIV maintenance drugs and other more widely used medications. Inevitably, an institutionalized homophobia and judgmental attitude about the acquired aspect of HIV also become a force in treatment availability.

Homophobia has played a significant role in the spread of HIV worldwide as well as within the smaller communities of Native peoples. I briefly touched on the ways in which Two-Spirit men are alienated by their communities due to homophobia. Also, I briefly touched upon the fact that the majority of gay Natives leave their communities and reservations to seek acceptance and tolerance for their differences. Many of the people who leave the reservation experience the sexual and social freedom that large urban gay communities provide. In their quest for sexual and social liberty, many Native peoples become involved in the "gay scene," which is well known to involve a considerable amount of substance abuse. Substance abuse combined with a longing for sexual freedom can lead to "risky behaviors" and potentially to HIV infection. Many people are thought to leave the reservation and rural communities with very little idea of the sexually related risk factors that are more prevalent in urban areas. Furthermore, they are also thought to spread sexually transmitted diseases among a naïve reservation population upon return visits.

The lack of open communication about sex, much less same-sex relations and gender difference, among Native communities is consistently recognized as a major factor in the spread of HIV among heterosexual, gay, bisexual, and lesbian Indians. The framing of HIV as a gay "white man's" disease has had a considerable impact on Native community perceptions. It is often noted that reservation and rural Native communities, because of their size and general geographic isolation, see themselves as immune to a disease explicitly associated with urban white gay populations.[2] I would suggest that the denial of differences such as same-sex relations among Native communities is explicitly tied to the lack of recognition for Native people's risk of HIV infection. That is, if there are no gay Indians, as some believe, then there is no risk of Native exposure to HIV.

The stories of those infected with HIV/AIDS are similar to many people who have experienced alienation from their tribal communities based on sexual orientation and gender difference. Some of the life experiences I observed centering around individual difference included people coming out to their families, families and friends accepting sex and gender difference, individuals learning of their HIV-positive status, and public acts of discrimination. However, I was most affected by the struggles of those who live daily life on the margins of death and deal with the alienation and uncertainty of their disease. During the course of my research, a couple of Two-Spirit people I knew died from complications due to AIDS, and a few others became critically ill and almost died. Infection, illness, and death are common topics of discussion, and in many ways become a part of Two-Spirit culture. Yet I came to learn that despite the localized nature of Native attitudes toward the HIV-infected, the socioeconomic and political aspects of HIV infection are involved in broader groups of individuals and are perpetuated by larger perceptions of difference.

In examining community reactions to HIV/AIDS, as well as to sexual orientation, it is important to recognize the ways difference becomes a set of experiences that can shape quality of life. Difference as a shaper of individual and collective experience can be seen across boundaries of culture, sex and gender, class, and race. Inevitably we have to ask, How do experiences of difference affect quality of life? And how does difference determine structured relationships in the contemporary world? As I have attempted to demonstrate here, difference is about more than representation. It is in fact a structuring quality that acts to socially, politically, and economically structure peoples' lives. Where there is no tolerance for difference, individuals suffer certain consequences. Two-Spirit people remind us that the consequences they face by identifying as Indian, tribally affiliated, gay, mixed blood, and transgender also have consequences for Indian peoples in general. That is, Two-Spirit people perceive the lack of acceptance for multiple kinds of difference among Indian communities as negating the continuation of Native culture as well as individual survivability.

After long conversations on issues of race, health, tribal politics, social participation, and just about anything Indian, Ben would always say in almost the form of a prayer, "We need to take care of our people." I came to figure out that behind Ben's statement was a desire to emphasize the multiple differences among Indian peoples as a political and social strategy, that is, difference as solidarity. In this way Two-Spirit people are actively engaged in a complex negotiation of social, political, and personal desires, much like mainstream Native society. They want the same things as other indigenous peoples such as equal opportunities to self-determination, maintenance of their social relations, and freedom in religion. Despite perceptions of alienation, are Two-Spirit people representative of Native Americans as a whole? Two-Spirit people would say yes. Although Two-Spirit people have no illusions about the recognition of same-sex relations or gender difference as solving all of Native America's problems, they do, however, see it as part of a larger solution, one that involves self-determination in reevaluating what it means to be a contemporary Indian person. The solution for them also involves challenging the hegemony of representations of Indians, as well as resisting the ways representation is used to create policies that affect the basic human existence of indigenous peoples.

Notes

1. I use the term "Two-Spirit" as the men in this book use it, which will become clearer and more specific as the book progresses. In this same way I use the term "gay" in preference to the word "homosexual," which is a problematic term used to discriminate against and pathologize same-sex relations.

2. A "lulu" is a trill where a person vibrates the tongue on the roof of the mouth to make a "lululu" noise. It is a form of expression commonly used by women to express approval or intensity of emotion. What is called "lulu-ing" is a common form of expression in Native culture in general.

3. Walter Williams's *The Spirit and the Flesh* (1986), Will Roscoe's *The Zuni Man-Woman* (1991) and *Changing Ones* (1998), and Sabine Lang's *Men as Women, Women as Men* (1998) fully and expertly document gender diversity among the majority of Native peoples in North America. Scholars have also pointed out that there were female-bodied persons who fulfilled third-gender categories. However, a great deal less is known about the female third gender. Sabine Lang (1998) gives the most attention to this topic, and Roscoe (1998) devotes a chapter to it.

4. In describing the historical institution of male-bodied persons, I will forgo the use of the term *berdaches* per Thomas and Jacobs (1999). Instead, I will use the terms *women-men* from Lang (1998), or *third-gender men*, for better understanding, because these signal both alternative gender status as well as bodily sex.

5. William Trexler (2002:9) argues that Natives "in effect were determining for an infant or young child, a gender that child could not possibly have arrived at by a free action of his other will." And, "Wherever we encounter parents or elders imposing gender upon children through such alleged tests, this is really an exercise in parental or other adult authority and not of the child's free will."

6. Early anthropological descriptions of the sexual behavior of third-

gender men are vague, with the exception of works by Devereaux (1937). For the most part, early anthropologists considered the gender mixing and sexuality of the "berdache" to be pathological and abhorrent. An example is George Catlin's description of the Sac and Fox "dance of the berdaches": "This is one of the most unaccountable and disgusting customs, that I have ever met in the Indian country . . . and where I should wish that it may be extinguished before it be more fully recorded" (1973:215). The famous anthropologist Alfred L. Kroeber's (1902) descriptions of Arapahoe *haxu'xan* sexuality are written in Latin, presumably to hide their explicit nature and get them past censors. These biases reduce possible conclusions to simply knowing that sexual relations between third-gender men and other men were recorded by anthropologists and travelers and were part of the local lore among some tribal peoples.

2. FROM GAY TO INDIAN

1. The 1969 riot at the Stonewall Inn, a gay social club in New York City, is considered the event that began the modern gay liberation movement.

2. I use "supratribal" and "supratribal consciousness" in the same way that Stephen Cornell (1988) uses them in *The Return of the Native.*

3. Reservations were broken up and allotted to individuals in the late 19th century after the U.S. Congress passed the General Allotment Act of 1887, also known as the Dawes Act. Because of the local Native population and tribal headquarters there, certain areas and cities in Oklahoma are associated with particular tribes, such as Tahlequah for the Cherokee and Anadarko for its association with the former Kiowa, Apache, Comanche reservation.

3. ADAPTING TO HOMOPHOBIA AMONG INDIANS

1. All the major works on Native gender diversity emphasize the ways in which some Two-Spirit people are accepted in their communities (Lang 1998; Roscoe 1991, 1998; Thomas and Jacobs 1999; Williams 1986). By emphasizing the rare occurrences of familial and community accep-

tance, they are ignoring the majority of Two-Spirit people who see themselves as not accepted in their tribal and local communities. Weston points out that "intellectual projects" on the institutionalization of variability in sexual practice and gender variation had as their goal to document and assess the degree of tolerance for homosexuality among "other" societies, and the correlation of social organization with same-sex relations and cross-cultural "typologies" of homosexuality (1993:342). Accordingly, by emphasizing historical manifestations of gender/sex difference acceptance, scholars mentioned here have eschewed the contemporary relationship between social belonging, acceptance, and desire in Native society. Studies of Native North American gender diversity have yet to ask, In what ways do dominant ideas about same-sex desire complicate Two-Spirit attempts at social and self-acceptance?

2. Hobsbawm characterizes these shifts, or "inventions" (I prefer "changes"), as follows: "We should expect it [change in what is perceived as tradition] to occur more frequently when a rapid transformation of society weakens or destroys the social patterns for which 'old' traditions had been designed, producing new ones to which they were not applicable, . . . when such old traditions and their institutional carriers . . . no longer prove sufficiently adaptable . . . or are otherwise eliminated" (1983:4).

3. Owls have connotations of bad luck in certain tribes, while others associate them in a positive way with transporting souls to the spirit world. They are almost universally seen as omens, negative or positive.

4. Walters provides some insight on being Indian and coming out: "The value of 'coming out' and being openly gay is valued as part of healthy psychosocial development among the gay and lesbian community. However, cooperation, a cultural value, emphasizes 'security in being a member of the group and in not being singled out and placed in a position above or below others.' The Indian value of cooperation is opposed to the gay and lesbian value of being individualistic and placing one's needs above the group and to self-identity as different and out. [Another] related value held by Indian peoples is to strive for anonymity where the needs of the group are considered over those of the

individual. Coming out requires one to openly identify oneself and draw attention to oneself, a process that is considered disrespectful within the Indian community" (1997:51). Walters's interpretation of the ways in which coming out is not part of Indian values makes a valid point. At the same time, it assumes that Two-Spirit men want to emphasize their "self-identity as different and out," while in actuality they go through considerable effort to emphasize their similarity with the Indian community by perfecting performances of identity. Therefore, they desire to be an equal part of the community. They also desire the anonymity that social incorporation brings. That is, they desire formal social roles in an Indian community where misapprehension about gayness is negated by the incorporation of difference.

5. Most Two-Spirit people use the term "out" to designate its gay meaning. I have used the term to designate a form of social and personal recognition that goes back and forth between Two-Spirit and non-gay Indian social worlds.

6. The *Kinaalda* is a Navajo coming-of-age ceremony for women. It is usually a multiday ceremony where a young girl is transformed from a child to a full, functioning adult member of the society (Frisbie 1993).

7. Becoming an alternate gender is documented in countless contact- and colonial-era writings and in early anthropological studies. Lang (1998), Roscoe (1998), and Williams (1986) provide extensive reviews of the documentation.

8. Rather, as Williams points out, "One merely accepted the child's non-masculinity as a part of the latent personality or potential with which the child had been endowed by nature. Since a third gender status was institutionalized in most of the Native American cultures . . . a radical divergence and subsequent chasm between sex of birth (i.e. biological sex) and chosen gender role was not regarded as deviant and so did not require an explanation" (1986:53).

9. Jacobs (1997) and Medicine (1997) note similar attitudes.

10. Foster 1991 details the ways that the Comanches attempt to save face for themselves and their families by not transcending cultural attitudes and mores. Shame is used similarly to avoid individuals drawing negative attention to their family members.

11. Beverly Little Thunder tells of her experiences: "As I became more deeply involved in the ceremonies of my people and began to participate in the Sun Dance Ceremony, I become more and more terrified of being 'found out.' I feared that if anyone knew of my desire to be with another woman I would be stricken from the ceremonies that were now such an important part of my life. My fears turned out to be real, but I never expected that the same people who taught me so much . . . would be some of those who would later reject me" (1997:206).

12. Timothy Sweet sees the emphasis on the hypermasculine warrior tradition as the result of "the masculine gendering of the self as a warrior and the US government policy, also enacted by 'warriors,' that sought to eliminate the Native American warrior tradition in order to control and ultimately eradicate tribal cultural wholes" (1995:220–222).

13. "Girls" or "girl" is a word that men in the popular gay community use to refer to one another.

14. "Camp" is a term used within the gay community and academia to refer to male parodist performances of exaggerated female mannerisms and language. Generally, camp behavior is reserved for social interactions in gay community contexts, and is assumed to evoke a negative reaction when used in "straight" social realms. According to Michasiw, "What is constructed by the camp-performative is a set of limits . . . fixing the viewers in ranges of ironic contract: those who do not know at all; those who think they know but do not; those who know, but only from without and are afraid really to know; those who do know but are appalled, or are laughing, or are laughing at the wrong pitch; and you. All of these limits depend, of course, on recognition on the part of the viewer but these reconditions are structured by the individual viewer's relative ignorance or knowledge of a stable set of codes and on the attitude characteristically struck by the viewer to that ignorance or knowledge" (1994:4).

15. Antonio Gramsci tells us that individuals who participate in the public social field where resources are exchanged "consent . . . to the general direction imposed on social life by the dominant fundamental group" (1971:12). Accordingly, by seeking access to symbolic resources, one is obligated to perform according to accepted and regulated com-

munity ideas. As we have seen so far, the community's ideas about Two-Spirit public performance have changed drastically through time, both in physical existence and perception. Consent to these changes is "historically caused by the prestige which the dominant group enjoys because of its position and function in the world of production" (Gramsci 1971:12). Through time, Two-Spirit identity became no longer available due to changes in the world of ideological production. Accordingly, these ideological shifts resulted in the alienation of certain individuals from Indian society. In denying the existence of Two-Spirit men, Indian communities "enforce discipline on those groups who do not 'consent' either actively or passively" (Gramsci 1971:12).

4. THE AESTHETICS OF AN IDENTITY

1. Although Jeff and Carl had a powwow-size drum in the car, we had been drinking and it would therefore have been inappropriate to sing at a drum often used for ceremony or powwows. As anyone familiar with 49s knows, car hoods, trash cans, and coolers are often used to replace drums in social drinking situations. Furthermore, the leader of the drum (coffee table) made certain that no powwow or ceremonial songs were sung because we had been consuming alcohol, despite the insistence on some favorite dance songs on the part of other singers. Stigma and the negative feelings about alcohol and Indians also play a significant role in the separation of the bar scene from practices considered traditional.

2. Two-Spirit as an identity making gay identity secondary is also mentioned by Lang (1998), Roscoe (1998), and Thomas and Jacobs (1999).

3. As previously pointed out by Thomas and Jacobs, "Two-spirit reflects the range of sexuality and gender identity derived from spiritual contemplation of one's place on this earth, this contemplation shored up by the teachings from parents and elders about how to live as a two-spirit person" (1999:95). Allen (1981), Jacobs et al. (1997), Lang (1998), Roscoe (1993, 1998), Williams (1986), and numerous other scholars emphasize the goal of recognizing Two-Spirit ("berdache" to some) iden-

tity as spiritual, thereby attempting to make it on the whole separate from sexuality and sexual practice, especially when conceived of in Euro-American terms.

4. Karina Walters (1997, 1998) has published extensively on Native GLBT issues concerning allegiances to one's racial identity and their sex/ gender identity.

5. Peyote stitch is a style and technique for beading cylindrical objects such as fan handles, dance sticks, and staffs.

6. Traditional looking is a way of describing an individual's appearance in comparison to popular ideas about the physical characteristics of historic Native peoples.

7. The emphasis placed on individual tribal affiliation was crucial in distinguishing Two-Spirits (and Indians) from non-Indian gays and wannabes. However, more importantly, tribal affiliation became an internal litmus test for authenticity in individuals' cultural beliefs and practices. Often in mainstream Indian society, conceptions of identity are tied to nationalist and essentialist interpretations of tribal identities (Sturm 1998, 2002). Sturm found that "Cherokee identity is socially and politically constructed around hegemonic notions of blood, color, race, and culture that permeate discourses of social belonging in the United States. . . . [R]acial ideologies have filtered from the national to the local level, where they have been internalized, manipulated, and resisted in different ways" (1998:230). Accordingly, dominant ideologies about what racial and cultural characteristics qualify as legitimately Indian, be that tribal or community affiliation, become "local" schemes in Two-Spirit identity. In this way, tribal identities crosscut Two-Spirit identity, creating a reliance on dominant racial ideologies for the inclusion and exclusion of individuals. For Two-Spirit people, these ideologies translate not only into a legitimate claim to tribal identity but also to community participation.

8. Jaimes and Halsey note the problematic appropriation of Indian traditions by "radical or lesbian feminists and gay male activists": "Particularly offensive have been non-Indian efforts to convert the indigenous custom of treating homosexuals as persons endowed with spe-

cial spiritual powers into a polemic for mass organization within the dominant society" (1992:333).

9. Historically, many North American tribes viewed menstruating women as potentially "contaminating" or disruptively powerful. For example, among some Siouan peoples and among the Mandans, Hidatsas, and Arikaras, menstruating women were segregated in separate tipis and not allowed to come into contact with men or men's implements of war and religion (Hassrick 1964:41, 124–125; Peters 2000:72). According to Frisbie, the Navajo see menstrual blood (and most blood for that matter) as unsanitary. Women are restricted in the tasks that they can perform and are sometimes segregated. They also feel that menstrual blood becomes more dangerous as a women gets older (1993:7–8, 351–353). Accordingly, most of the Two-Spirit men I knew and interviewed adhered to their tribally specific taboos about coming into contact with food cooked by women who were menstruating, as well as sharing sleeping quarters or ceremonial space with them.

5. CULTURAL COMPROMISE AT WORK

1. It is widely accepted among Two-Spirit people that the Lakota *winkte* was one of the last culturally intact mixed-gender statuses to exist into the 20th century. While I knew several people who identified themselves as winkte, during my research I never met anyone who had specifically identified roles as a winkte in their community. I frequently heard rumors and legends of winktes with community-sanctioned roles in the Sun Dance and other contexts on the Pine Ridge and Rosebud reservations. Walter Williams (1986) notes contemporary public roles for winktes among the Lakota.

2. To arrive at this notion of gender, the Two-Spirit people of the last 15 years have no doubt drawn upon the theoretical works on Native gender of Will Roscoe and Walter Williams.

3. See Jackson (2003) for a recent discussion of the significance of the Stomp Dance.

4. Young men learning to lead will often wear shells to increase their knowledge and ability. However, they would never wear shells in a com-

munity Stomp Dance ceremony, as that would be seen as a woman's role.

5. The "lavender lexicon" is a phrase often used to describe gay men's speech as it reflects gay community speech patterns (Leap 1995; Zwicky 1997).

6. "Miss Denver AIDS Coalition" is a fictitious title.

7. Powwow emcees are often given gifts of cash or items such as blankets for their services. These are seen as payments in the form of honoring the person for their work.

6. MENDING THE HOOP

1. Paula Gunn Allen uses mending the hoop as a metaphor in her feminist critique of the treatment of women (1981). In Allen's way the hoop represents the whole of Indian society as thrown off balance by the decline in women's status and by the lack of empowerment for Native women (1981). Therefore, Native society is out of balance because respect for women is missing. Allen argues that women must become respected for Native society to be whole again.

2. Roscoe (1998:107) and Two-Spirit informants have pointed out that the "de-gaying" of HIV/AIDS issues has the potential to counter the work done to create awareness in gay and non-gay communities.

7. DIFFERENCE AND SOCIAL BELONGING

1. Because of the nature of Zach's disclosure, I am not identifying him as a member of a particular Two-Spirit group.

2. Baldwin et al. (1996), Greeley (1995), and Weaver (1999) all point to images of white urban gay males as the ethnic stereotype for HIV-infected individuals.

Works Cited

Allen, Paula Gunn
   1981 – Lesbians in American Indian Cultures. Conditions 7:67–87.
Altman, Dennis
   1979 – Coming Out in the Seventies. Sydney: Wild and Woolley Press.
Baldwin, Julie A., John E. Rolf, Jeanette Johnson, and Jeremy Bowers
   1996 – Developing Culturally Sensitive HIV/AIDS and Substance
   Abuse Prevention Curricula for Native American Youth. Journal of
   School Health 66(9):322–327.
Basso, Keith
   1979 – Portraits of the Whiteman. Cambridge: Cambridge Univer-
   sity Press.
Bernstein, Mary
   1997 – Celebration and Suppression: The Strategic Uses of Identity
   by the Lesbian and Gay Movement. American Journal of Sociology
   103(3):531–565.
Blackwood, Evelyn
   1984 – Sexuality and Gender in Certain Native American Tribes:
   The Case of Cross-gender Females. Signs: Journal of Women in
   Culture and Society 10(1):27–42.
Bowers, Alfred W.
   1965 – Hidatsa Social and Ceremonial Organization. Smithsonian
   Institution Bureau of American Ethnology Bulletin 194. Washington DC: U.S. Government Printing Office.
Burns, Randy
   1988 – Preface. In Living the Spirit: A Gay American Indian Anthol-
   ogy. Will Roscoe, ed. Pp. i–vii. New York: St. Martin's Press.
Butler, Judith
   1990 – Gender Trouble: Feminism and the Subversion of Identity.
   New York: Routledge.
   1992 – Contingent Foundations: Feminism and the Question of
   "Postmodernism." In Feminists Theorize the Political. J. Butler and
   J. W. Scott, eds. New York: Routledge.

1993 – Bodies that Matter. New York: Routledge.

Callender, Charles, and Lee M. Kochems

1983 – The North American Berdache. Current Anthropology 24(2):443–470.

Cameron, Deborah, and Don Kulick

2003 – Language and Sexuality. Cambridge: Cambridge University Press.

Catlin, George

1973 [1844] – Letters and Notes on the Manners, Customs, and Conditions of the North American Indians. New York: Dover Publications.

Cornell, Stephen

1988 – The Return of the Native: American Indian Political Resurgence. New York: Oxford University Press.

Deloria, Phillip J.

1998 – Playing Indian. New Haven: Yale University Press.

d'Emilio, John

1992 – Making Trouble: Essays on Gay History, Politics, and the University. New York: Routledge.

Devereaux, George

1937 – Institutionalized Homosexuality of the Mohave Indians. Human Biology 9:498–523.

Dozier, Edward P.

1958 – Spanish-Catholic Influences on Rio Grande Pueblo Religion. American Anthropologist 60(3):441–448.

1964 – The Pueblo Indians of the Southwest. Current Anthropology 5(2):79–97.

Edwards, Jeffrey

2000 – AIDS, Race, and the Rise and Decline of a Militant Oppositional Lesbian and Gay Politics in the U.S. New Political Science 22(4):485–506.

Epple, Carolyn

1998 – Coming to Terms with Navajo Nadleehi: A Critique of Berdache, Gay, Alternate Gender and Two-Spirit. American Ethnologist 25(2):267–290.

Epstein, Steven

    1987 – Gay Politics, Ethnic Identity: The Limits of Social Construc-
tionism. Socialist Review 93/94 (July–September 1987): 9–54.

Foster, Morris W.

    1991 – Being Comanche. Tucson: University of Arizona Press.

Foucault, M.

    1978 – The History of Sexuality, vol. 1: An Introduction.
Harmondsworth UK: Penguin.

    1986 – The History of Sexuality, vol. 3: The Care of the Self.
Harmondsworth UK: Penguin.

    1988 – Technologies of the Self. *In* Technologies of the Self: A Semi-
nar with Michel Foucault. Luther H. Martin, Huck Gutman, and
Patrick H. Hutton, eds. Pp. 16–49. Amherst: University of Massa-
chusetts Press.

    1990 – The History of Sexuality, vol. 2: The Use of Pleasure.
Harmondsworth UK: Penguin.

Frisbie, Charlotte Johnson

    1993 [1967] – Kinaalda: A Study of the Navaho Girl's Puberty Cer-
emony. Salt Lake City: University of Utah Press.

Goulet, Jean-Guy A.

    1996 – The 'Berdache'/'Two-Spirit': A Comparison of Anthropo-
logical and Native Constructions of Gendered Identities Among
the Northern Athapaskans. Journal of Royal Anthropological Institute, n.s., 2:683–701.

Gramsci, Antonio

    1995 [1971] – Selections from the Prison Notebooks. New York: In-
ternational Publishers.

Greeley, Alexandra

    1995 – Concern about AIDS in Minority Communities. FDA Con-
sumer 29:11–15.

Harvey, Keith

    1998 – Translating Camp Talk: Gay Identities and Cultural Transfer.
The Translator 4(2):295–320

    2000 – Describing Camp Talk: Language/Pragmatics/Politics. Lan-
guage and Literature 9(3):240–260.

Hassrick, Royal B.

    1964 – The Sioux. Norman: University of Oklahoma Press.

Hobsbawm, Eric

    1983 – Introduction: Inventing Traditions. *In* The Invention of Tradition. Eric Hobsbawm and Terence Ranger, eds. Pp. 1–14. Cambridge: Cambridge University Press.

Hoebel, E. Adamson

    1960 – The Cheyennes. New York: Holt, Rinehart and Winston.

Jackson, Jason Baird

    2000 – Signaling the Creator: Indian Football as Ritual Performance among the Yuchi and Their Neighbors. Southern Folklore 57(1):33–64.

    2003 – Yuchi Ceremonial Life. Lincoln: University of Nebraska Press.

Jacobs, Sue-Ellen

    1997 – Is the North American Berdache Merely a Phantom in the Imagination of Western Social Scientists? *In* Two-Spirit People: Gender Identity, Sexuality, and Spirituality. Sue-Ellen Jacobs, Wesley Thomas, and Sabine Lang, eds. Pp. 21–44. Chicago: University of Illinois Press.

Jacobs, Sue Ellen, Wesley Thomas (Navajo), and Sabine Lang

    1997 – Introduction. *In* Two-Spirit People: Native American Gender Identity, Sexuality, and Spirituality. Sue-Ellen Jacobs, Wesley Thomas, and Sabine Lang, eds. Pp. 1–20. Chicago: University of Illinois Press.

Jaimes, M. Annette, and Theresa Halsey

    1992 – American Indian Women: At the Center of Indigenous Resistance in Contemporary North America. *In* The State of Native America: Genocide, Colonization, and Resistance. M. Annette Jaimes, ed. Pp. 311–344. Boston: South End Press.

Kroeber, Alfred L.

    1902 [1983] – The Arapaho. Lincoln: University of Nebraska Press.

    1940 – Psychosis or Social Sanction? Character and Personality 3(3):204–215.

Kulick, Don

    1998 – Travesti. Chicago: University of Chicago Press.

Lang, Sabine

1997 – Various Kinds of Two-Spirit People: Gender Variance and
Homosexuality in Native American Communities. *In* Two-Spirit
People: Gender Identity, Sexuality, and Spirituality. Sue-Ellen
Jacobs, Wesley Thomas, and Sabine Lang, eds. Pp. 100–118. Chicago:
University of Illinois Press.

1998 – Men as Women, Women as Men. Austin: University of Texas
Press.

Leap, William

1995 – Word's Out: Gay Men's English. Minneapolis: University of
Minnesota Press.

Little Thunder, Beverly

1997 – I Am a Lakota Woman. *In* Two-Spirit People: Native American Gender Identity, Sexuality, and Spirituality. Sue-Ellen Jacobs,
Wesley Thomas, and Sabine Lang, eds. Pp. 203–209. Chicago: University of Illinois Press.

Lowie, Robert H.

1912 – Social Life of the Crow Indians. Anthropological Papers of
the American Museum of Natural History, vol. 9, pt. 2. New York:
Order of the Trustees.

Mattern, Mark

1996 – The Powwow as a Public Arena for Negotiating Unity and
Diversity in American Indian Life. American Indian Culture and
Research Journal 20(4):183–201.

McLeod, Albert

1998 – 11th Annual International Two-Spirit Gathering: A Project
Report by the Manitoba Aboriginal AIDS Task Force. Winnipeg
MB: Manitoba Aboriginal AIDS Task Force, Inc. (MAATF).

Medicine, Beatrice (Standing Rock Lakota)

1997 – Changing Native American Roles in an Urban Context and
Changing Native American Sex Roles in an Urban Context. *In*
Two-Spirit People: Native American Gender Identity, Sexuality, and
Spirituality. Sue-Ellen Jacobs, Wesley Thomas, and Sabine Lang,
eds. Pp. 145–155. Chicago: University of Illinois Press.

Michasiw, Kim

1994 – Camp, Masculinity, Masquerade. differences: A Journal of Feminist Cultural Studies 6(2-3):146–170.

Peters, Virginia Bergman

2000 – Women of the Earth Lodges. Norman: University of Oklahoma Press.

Roscoe, Will

1991 – The Zuni Man-Woman. Albuquerque: University of New Mexico Press.

1993 – How to Become a Berdache: Toward a Unified Analysis of Gender Diversity. *In* Third Sex, Third Gender. G. Herdt, ed. Pp. 329–372. New York: Zone Books.

1998 – Changing Ones. New York: St. Martin's Press.

Victoria Sanchez

2001 – Intertribal Dance and Cross Cultural Communication: Traditional Powwows in Ohio. Communication Studies 52(1):51–72.

Schaeffer, Claude E.

1965 – The Kutenai Female Berdache. Ethnohistory 12(3):193–236.

Scott, James

1985 – Weapons of the Weak. New Haven: Yale University Press.

1990 – Domination and the Arts of Resistance. New Haven: Yale University Press.

Sturm, Circe

1998 – Blood Politics, Racial Classification, and Cherokee National Identity: The Trials and Tribulations of the Cherokee Freedman. American Indian Quarterly 22(1-2):230–258.

2002 – Blood Politics: Race, Culture, and Identity in the Cherokee Nation of Oklahoma. Berkeley: University of California Press.

Sweet, Timothy

1995 – Masculinity and Self-Performance in the Life of Black Hawk. *In* Subjects and Citizens: Nation, Race, and Gender from Oroonoko to Anita Hill. Michael Moon and Cathy Davidson, eds. Pp. 219–244. Durham NC: Duke University Press.

Thomas, Wesley (Navajo)

1997 – Navajo Cultural Constructions of Gender and Sexuality. *In*

Two-Spirit People: Native American Gender Identity, Sexuality and Spirituality. Sue-Ellen Jacobs, Wesley Thomas, and Sabine Lang, eds. Pp. 156–173. Chicago: University of Illinois Press.

Thomas, Wesley, and Sue-Ellen Jacobs

1999 – ". . . And We Are Still Here": From Berdache to Two-Spirit People. American Indian Culture and Research Journal 23(2):91–107.

Trexler, Richard

1995 – Sex and Conquest. Ithaca NY: Cornell University Press.

2002 – Making the American Berdache: Choice or Constraint? Journal of Social History 35(3):613–636.

Walters, Karina

1997 – Urban Lesbian and Gay American Indian Identity: Implications for Mental Health Service Delivery. *In* Two Spirit People: American Indian Lesbian Women and Gay Men. Lester B. Brown, ed. Pp. 43–65. New York: Haworth Press.

1998 – Negotiating Conflicts in Allegiances among Lesbians and Gays of Color: Reconciling Divided Selves and Communities. *In* Foundations of Social Work Practice with Lesbians and Gay Persons. Gerald P. Mallon, ed. Pp. 46–75. New York: Haworth Press.

Weaver, Hillary N.

1999 – Through Indigenous Eyes: Native Americans and the HIV Epidemic. Health and Social Work 24(1):27–34.

Weston, Kath

1993 – Lesbian/Gay Studies in the House of Anthropology. Annual Reviews in Anthropology 22:339–367.

Whitehead, Harriet

1993 – The Bow and the Burden Strap: A New Look at Institutionalized Homosexuality in Native North America. *In* The Lesbian and Gay Studies Reader. H. Abelove, M. Barale, and D. Halperin, eds. Pp. 498–527. New York: Routledge.

Williams, Walter L.

1986 – The Spirit and the Flesh: Sexual Diversity in American Indian Culture. New York: Beacon Press.

Womack, Craig

   1999 – Red on Red: Native American Literary Separatism. Minneapolis: University of Minnesota Press.

Zwicky, Arnold M.

   1997 – Two Lavender Issues for Linguists. *In* Queerly Phrased: Language, Gender, and Sexuality. A. Livia and K. Hall, eds. New York: Oxford University Press.

Index